Life Out Of Reach

Spare Burden

By

Jas Dosanjh

Published by Jasvir Dosanjh
www.jasdosanjh.com

A CIP catalogue record for this title is available from the British Library.

Paperback ISBN 978-1-912510-06-1
Kindle ISBN 978-1-912510-07-8

Life Out Of Reach, Spare Burden – Jas Dosanjh
2nd Edition

Editing by W. Boggess, New York Editors
Cover Design Concept – Jas Dosanjh

CONTENTS

A Note from the Author

This book is based on true events. All characters, incidents and dialogues are real, though names and minor details have been changed to protect identities. The therapy dialogues are based on my sessions with my therapist which have spanned several years. For ease of story-telling, the therapy sessions have been consolidated and summarized. The language most spoken in my home is Punjabi, however I have translated the dialogue into English. The conversations in this book come from my recollections and the recollections of those members of my family who helped clarify events. This book is not intended to hurt or embarrass any members of my family, but it is inevitable and regrettable that some feelings may be hurt.

Dedicated to my dad

When I told my dad that I was writing a book about my life, he looked horrified. He opened his mouth, but closed it again without saying a word. Then with great care and diligence, he set about helping me with dates, answering all of my questions to the best of his recollection and confirming many of my earliest memories. Without his help, this book would have been harder to write nor would it have been written so freely.

Acknowledgments

Simran and Rohan for reading the first few chapters and demanding to know what happened next – your desire to know more made me continue writing. My sisters and cousins for your love and understanding through both the funny chapters and the heart-breaking ones. Anna, Becky, Cheryl, Debbie, Ele, Maurice, Phil, Sareeta, Sophia and Venera for your encouragement and support. My therapist – without you I would have sunk long ago.

Prologue

The Settee Was Empty

'The bride's just fainted!'

Gasps of shock echoed through the congregation as my sixteen year old aunt Pally lay slumped and unconscious in front of the Guru Granth Sahib, the holy scripture of Sikhs. Her red wedding sari crumbled and creased as it puffed around her limp body. Her head drooped to one side and her gold jewellery, still glittering under the bright lights of Willenhall Sikh gurdwara was tangled around her forehead.

Wedding guests strained their necks and some even stood to get a better glimpse. I was seated next to my mother who, along with the rest of my worried family, rushed to help. As relatives crowded at Pally's side, the stunned congregation became subdued.

'Someone get a glass of water! Hurry!' said Bhav, Pally's older sister as she cradled Pally's head in her arms. 'Pally! Pally! What's wrong? Wake up!' As a glass of cold water arrived, Bhav frantically splashed droplets onto her sister's face.

Moments earlier, standing alongside her groom, Pally had been preparing for the first part of her wedding ceremony. All was proceeding as it should have been, when suddenly she'd wobbled, swayed and collapsed down to the floor.

I fixed my eyes on my fallen aunt. My heart went out to the helpless figure on the floor of the gurdwara. I hoped that Pally fainting would stop the wedding from going ahead and we could all go home. Pally had seemed to accept that her adult life would begin by her being married off to a complete stranger, but maybe now that her wedding was actually happening, she was reluctant and scared. Maybe that was why she had fainted.

Pally's marriage had been arranged by the men in our family - her father (my paternal grandfather) and her older brothers. She had had no say in the man that they'd chosen for her. Their only objective had been to get her married off as soon as it was legally possible.

I didn't understand marriage. Even at the age of ten, I felt a profound sense of suffocation at the thought of marriage. A feeling I quietly learnt to control and suppress because all around me, the expectation from my family and relatives was that 'of course a girl gets married - what else was there for her to do?' According to all of the women in my large extended family, there was nothing in a girl's future apart from marriage. Any feelings of unwillingness or reluctance on the part of the bride would be overridden and crushed by the enthusiasm of her relatives. Swallowed up by the noise, hum-drum and excitement of planning a big Punjabi wedding, running alongside would be an undercurrent of relief that the burden of a daughter was now passing onto another family. However as I watched the muddle of people standing over Pally, I felt there was something else.

As a dazed Pally slowly came round, she mumbled an explanation. 'M-my mother was here . . . I saw Mama. I saw her and then . . . I just saw this darkness and everything went black.'

My family exchanged brief glances across Pally's head, but stayed silent as they helped her sit up.

As news of Pally's explanation spread through the congregation, the wedding guests began to shift nervously. Their eyes filled with unease and disbelief as they anxiously glanced around. They began whispering that Pally was imagining things. She couldn't possibly have seen her mother because Mama had died eight years earlier.

My family tried to restore calm among the bewildered and nervous guests and reassured the alarmed groom and his family that Pally was not crazy or suffering from hallucinations. Gradually the spooked congregation settled into tense murmurings. As Pally composed herself, two additional women were brought forward to assist her through the long ceremony.

My dad insisting that the priest continue. 'Please carry on . . . she's fine now, nothing happened. We want to get on with the ceremony without any more delay.'

With a cautious look in his eyes, the befuddled priest agreed to restart the wedding ceremony from the beginning. But even as the wedding guests continued to whisper that Pally had been imagining things, my family and I knew that she'd been telling the truth. We were accustomed to such strange occurrences, aware that certain members of our family had the gift to sense the dead. Pally had frequently been visited by our ancestors, something that she feared and disliked.

The second eldest daughter of Sikh Punjabi parents, I had been born with the same gift, in addition to which I had an intuition that ran deeper than most peoples. Perhaps because I was a different kind of person to Pally, I didn't mind getting fleeting visits from those who had passed away, especially if I happened to sense the presence of Mama. She didn't visit often, so I learnt to cherish the brief short moments when she did.

Mama was my paternal grandmother and my earliest childhood memories were of her lying on the settee covered with a blanket. Even as a young child, I'd known that she was very ill. She'd never fully recovered after the birth of her youngest daughter Navi. Mama had begged and pleaded with my grandfather to allow her to return home to India, but he'd refused and she had remained bed-bound in Wolverhampton for the rest of her days.

Born in 1973, I was not the youngest child in the family, but I was Mama's favourite. She didn't pay much attention to the rest of her grandchildren, but she would tuck me under her blanket, giving me sweets and hugs. I would smile and giggle, feeling completely happy in her warm embrace.

When I was two and a half, I clambered over to where Mama should have been, but the settee was empty. Watching the settee, I sat and waited for her to return. She'd always been there and I couldn't understand where she had gone. I felt as if all of my happiness had been snatched away. For days afterwards, I would return to the settee, expecting her to be there, to make everything ok again.

Several months passed, then together with my grandfather and my dad's brothers and sisters, we all moved from our small terrace house in Wolverhampton into a semi-detached three bedroom house in Bentley. I refused to leave the old house until I'd searched the bare and empty rooms for Mama, distraught that she'd be left behind. I cried inconsolably as my dad picked me up and carried me out of the house and into the car waiting to take us to our new home. It was then, on that car journey that I finally realised that Mama had gone, though I didn't know where. And though Mama had left us first, I couldn't help but feel that we'd abandoned her by moving to a new house.

After she died, my grandmother was rarely spoken about. Though my parents tried to answer any questions

I had, they were vague about her death. I'm sure the doctors must have explained the exact cause of death to my family, but maybe the specifics were lost in translation from English to Punjabi. Decades after Mama died, I managed to get a copy of her death certificate and discovered that her cause of death was kidney failure. She was only forty-eight.

In hospital the evening she died, Mama had begged my grandfather and my dad to take her home. Pleading for them to get her out of the hospital, she was hysterical. Crying that if she stayed, she would be dead before the morning came. Dismissing her concerns and with visiting hours over, my grandfather and my dad left her at the hospital and drove home. They had only just walked into the house and shut the front door behind them when there was a loud knock at the door they had just closed. It was the police. We did not have a telephone so they had been dispatched to inform Mama's next-of-kin that she had died.

On Pally's wedding day, I'd felt Mama's presence in the gurdwara. But instead of giving me comfort as she usually did, she left me with a feeling of dark hopelessness. Shortly after her wedding, Pally's husband accidentally killed a motorcyclist in a tragic car accident. He spent time in prison for the crash, but his marriage to Pally ended shortly after his release. The ink was barely dry on her divorce papers before my family arranged for Pally to be shipped off and married to a Sikh Punjabi man who lived in Germany. Another husband she didn't have any say in.

'Those are very powerful memories to have Jas,' said my therapist. 'Before the age of three you'd experienced loss and grief. You learnt about endings at a young age.'

'Yeah, but being so young, I had no words to express my sadness. I just had this emotional void as well as a physical one because my grandmother was just gone. I learnt that there's always going to be an ending to every relationship

we have. Either someone dies and they leave you or they walk out of the door.'

'That's a sad way to think of relationships.'

'But that's how I felt and that's how I still feel. I think that's why I try not to get really attached to anyone because I always see the ending . . . like what's the point? However good or bad it is, it'll come to an end anyway.'

'Is that really how you think of relationships Jas?'

I nodded. 'Whenever I think about being in a relationship, in my mind I see a couple on a journey in a car. Sooner or later they're going to be approaching a cliff that they can't avoid driving off. Because one of them will die or one of them will leave. It's inevitable.'

'You don't think that the journey in the car may be long and beautiful?'

I shook my head. 'I find that thought almost impossible. I think because of my own experience and things I've seen happen in other people's relationships, I think relationships are horrible, controlling and suffocating, no one is happy or fulfilled. Especially not the women. So why would anyone want to get into that car in the first place? It's better to stay unattached if one can help it.'

'You were very attached to your grandmother though Jas.'

'I was - and then look what happened. She died and I've been in pain for most of my life because she left. It's the way she died as well that adds to the pain. If she was going to die anyway because she was so ill, they should have brought her home so she'd have been surrounded by family, instead of nurses who were strangers to her and who didn't even speak the same language. The only time I've ever seen my dad cry is when he talks about Mama's last few hours and how she begged him and his father to take her home from the hospital and how she told them again and again that she was going to die before the morning if they left her there. She predicted her own death, but they'd just ignored her. It's one of my dad's biggest regrets that he left her at the hospital.'

'Do you think your life would've been different if your grandmother had lived longer?'

'Without a doubt, she'd always have looked out for me.'

'And your grandfather? You haven't really spoken about him Jas.'

I shrugged and focused on the books lining the wooden shelf. 'What's there to say? He was a horrible man. He hated me and my sisters and he hated my parents because they only had daughters. He would punch the coffee table and shout at my parents because they didn't have any sons. He was just an angry, abusive man!'

One

Not A Man

'I saw her with my own eyes standing there talking to that man! That new neighbour! Do you know what she's been up to?' With a wooden rolling pin swinging in one hand, eyes wild and frothing at the mouth, standing over my trembling mother, my grandfather shouted at my dad. 'Do you? Because I saw what she was up to! I've beaten her already . . . now here, you take it!' My grandfather handed the rolling pin to my dad as he stepped back and sneered. 'She's your wife and you need to sort her out! She's been talking to that man from next door . . . that stranger! How dare she speak to him when she knows he's not a man from our family!'

A young man from India had moved in next door and my mother had been talking to him over the garden fence. She was keen to hear news of India and she'd been telling the new neighbour about the nearby shops and the local area.

'Stop this!' From where she was lying on the settee, Mama tried to intervene, but my grandfather ignored her. Unable to stand without assistance, Mama began pleading with her son. 'Daljit, don't you hit her! Put down that rolling pin! Don't hit her . . . don't you touch her Daljit! Why aren't you listening to me? Listen to me . . . let her go!'

My dad turned the rolling pin over in his hands and ignoring Mama's pleas, he turned to my mother who was shaking and sobbing. Without speaking or looking directly at her, my dad stepped forward and swung his arm back and brought the rolling pin down. My mother put up her arms to protect herself, but she was powerless to stop the force of my dad's blows. Her screams were echoed by Mama as her body was battered with the rolling pin and she crumbled down to the floor.

As soon as my mother fell to the ground, my dad stopped swinging and threw the rolling pin down next to her. 'Don't ever speak to a man who is not one of our relatives again! Do you understand?' And he stormed out.

As Mama wailed and cursed, my mother lay where she'd fallen on the floor of the living room. Crumbled up in pain, she wept as my grandfather snorted. 'Do you see what happens when you behave like a whore? I'm not having a whore in my house, dragging my family name down!'

As my mother struggled to get onto her feet and into the relative safety of the kitchen, my grandfather barked at her. 'And don't forget to pick up the rolling pin and take it with you, you won't be able to do any cooking without it!'

Without a word and trying to control her sobbing, with her head down, my mother picked up the rolling pin and stumbled out of the room.

'Instead of going into the kitchen, she should have picked up the rolling pin and smacked it over my grandfather's head! The very notion is so stupid that there are no words for it! Perhaps the sky is going to fall down because your wife spoke to another man! The world is going to end!

What does it even fucking mean if your wife talks to another man? That she's going to open her legs for him? Why the fuck don't men get beaten when they talk to a woman who is not their wife?'

'You sound very angry Jas and who can blame you.'

'It's because of the nonsense and bullshit of Indian culture and Sikh Punjabi men. They can be such hypocrites. More than once, when my mother had been washing up, my grandfather had come up behind her and tried to grope her and she'd had to push him off. The double standards don't even surprise me, what surprises me is that it's gone unchecked for so many centuries. My grandfather is proof that while you can take the man out of India, you can't take the Indian out of the man!'

Two

Handsome Enough

'Dada.' I held out my arms as my dad reached down and swung me up. Tucked safely in his arms, I pointed down at the neighbour's dog. On one side, we had white neighbours who kept a huge bulldog. He rarely barked, but he would growl and scratch at the flimsy wooden fence as he tried to get under it.

From the great height of my dad's arms, I watched as my older sister Dimple played with my aunts, Pally and Navi in our tiny back garden.

My mother emerged from the outside lavatory. 'I've just cleaned the toilet and put some bleach in it, so try not to use it for a while. I better take the clothes off the washing line before it gets dark.'

Gently squeezing one of my cheeks with his hand, my dad told my mother that he would be going to the pub with his brothers and his father.

Sighing my mother began to take the clothes off the washing line as my dad carried me into the house.

Finding my baby walker in a corner, he carefully placed me into it. As a baby, I had cried all the time until became distraught about how the villagers were taking advantage of her young son's easy-going nature, working him from dawn to dusk. Eventually she put her foot down and refused to allow any of the villagers to use my dad as free child labour. She was relieved when my grandfather left his British Army regiment in India and decided to move to England and take my dad with him.

My grandfather arrived in England in 1963 with £26 in his pocket and his two eldest sons, my dad Daljit and uncle Manjeet in tow. They moved in with relatives who had already settled in Wolverhampton and they helped my grandfather find work at a local foundry. Though still a teenager, my dad also went to work at the same foundry and he enrolled in evening classes at the local college to learn English. My uncle Manjeet went to secondary school for a couple of years, but when he reached the age of fifteen, he left and also started working in the same foundry as his father and his older brother. With all three of them earning, they saved enough so that my grandfather was able to bring Mama and the rest of his children over from India.

A few years later in 1971, my mother came to England and within a week of her arrival, she and my dad had a Sikh wedding ceremony at the local gurdwara. While my dad was surrounded by his family, having left all of her family behind in India, my mother had no one to call her own.

After they finished their day jobs at the foundry, in the evenings my dad and uncles would also pull pints at the local pub, The Red Lion. But pints weren't the only thing that they pulled. My uncles, who were even more handsome than my dad, would frequently get asked out by the white women who came into the pub.

But my grandfather hadn't come to England for romance. When two white women followed one of my uncles home and knocked on our front door asking for him, my grandfather who had opened the door, shouted at them in Punjabi. He was so furious that these white women had had the nerve to ask for one of his sons that he chased them down the road. Slamming the door shut as he came back in, my grandfather had huffed around the house, muttering about 'trashy white women,' but his complaints were punctuated by a few loud and satisfied grunts. He'd taught his sons well and they weren't stupid, they knew never to trust or interact with a white person unless there was an absolute need.

'My mother's life was hard. She was poor, uneducated, had too many children and lived in a small, cramped, overcrowded terrace house with ten other people in a foreign country. My dad worked hard at his job, but none of the men ever helped out with the chores or with us kids. Like most men of my dad's generation, they just expected to be fed, their clothes washed and ironed and the house spotless because you know . . . there's a fairy that does all of that! My mother also had to look after Mama who was very ill and Mama's seven children. My dad's family was huge – there was his older sister Pupinder, then my dad who's the oldest son, then came my aunt Bhav, my uncle Manjeet, my uncle Sandeep, my uncle Taran, my aunt Pally and then my dad's youngest sister, Navi who's only four years older than I am. My grandfather had eight children. Well . . . he had more, but he'd disposed of some of 'em in India as soon as they'd been born.'

'Disposed?'

'Yeah you know . . . strangled, drowned, suffocated.' I stopped and glanced at my therapist's face. 'Maybe I shouldn't be so casual about it, but I've grown up knowing that girls are unwanted and they'll be gotten rid of; either when they're born or they'll be married off to someone at the earliest opportunity. My parents never made any secret of the fact that they would've preferred to have had boys instead of girls. It's just part and parcel of my culture, so it's not a shock for me to hear of something like this happening in my own family. My grandfather treated me

and my sisters like vermin and I'm sure if we'd been born in India, my grandfather would've pressured my parents to get rid of us.'

'But you and your five sisters were all born here?'

I nodded. 'Looking back I don't know how my parents managed to settle in a strange country all those years ago without knowing the language, the areas, the laws or the people. Though they were never worried that they didn't know the people . . . they didn't want to know the people. We were always told that white people were untrustworthy.'

'Do you believe that white people are untrustworthy Jas?'

'I wasn't encouraged to have white friends, but I've had more help from white people than anyone else.'

Three

What's The Time, Mr Wolf?

'Have you seen how long her hair is?'

'Look at her pigtails! Watch me . . . I'm gonna pull 'em!'

Jostling against each other, a group of white boys were trying to grab my two pigtails.

I'd started school a few days earlier. The school building was a temporary solution, known fondly among the locals as 'the cowsheds' because it resembled a barn. It didn't have a dining hall so at dinnertime children would have to walk down the road to another school, King Charles Primary. A new school, County Bridge Primary was being built to replace 'the cowsheds,' but in the meantime children of all different ages were taught together in 'the cowsheds' three old classrooms.

The big playground at the front of the school was only for the older children, but I'd wandered into it and caught the attention of a group of boys. Suddenly finding myself stuck in a crowd of strange and unfriendly faces, I looked around for a way out as they began to swing their arms, trying to grab my hair. I realised that to get away I'd have to push past them, but there were too many of them and they were beginning to close in.

My eyes started to fill with tears and I could feel my bottom lip begin to wobble when suddenly two hands gripped me firmly around my waist and lifted me off my feet and straight up into the air. I was carried over the heads of the boys and in the blink of an eye, I was outside of their frightening circle.

'Are you ok Jas?' It was Daniel, my uncle Sandeep's best friend. He had seen what was happening and rushed over. Daniel was one of the oldest boys in the school and he towered over everyone else. He held onto me as he leaned towards the boys. 'Oi! If I ever see any of you trying to push her like that again, I'm gonna kick your faces in!' The boys immediately scattered, scampering in different directions.

'You alright?' Daniel turned to check if I was crying.

To me, Daniel seemed as tall and as strong as a giant. I shyly gave a small nod. 'I'm ok.'

'Come on, I'll keep an eye on you.' Daniel started to walk through the playground, but we'd only gone a few steps when my uncle Sandeep emerged from a crowd of playing children. He frowned as he spotted us and Daniel immediately set me down.

'Some boys were trying to pull her hair and I picked her up!' He explained to Sandeep.

My uncle glanced down at me as I stood quietly next to Daniel. 'Jas, this playground is only for us big children. Go round to the small playground and don't come back over here, ok?'

Grateful to have been rescued, leaving Daniel and my uncle, I wandered around to the small playground behind the school building.

Daniel always made a point of watching over me, even more than my uncles and aunts. Once when I'd been trying to make a daisy chain, he'd wandered over to help me. Other girls wanted him to make them daisy chains as well and as they'd vied for his attention, I was elbowed aside. I wandered off to play on my own, but Daniel soon made me come back and sit down next to him while he was stuck making countless daisy chains. Some days I would be playing on my own and I'd turn around and there he would be, standing there quietly watching me. I didn't mind because I knew that if he was there, then I wouldn't get picked on by any of the other children.

A few days later, crouching in the small playground I was playing with some twigs that I'd found when one of my classmates raced over. Slightly out of breath, she panted. 'Do you want to play What's The Time, Mr Wolf?'

I looked up from my pile of twigs. I didn't know what the game was, but happy to be included, I nodded. My classmate grabbed my hand and together we skipped over to where the other children were already playing. The rules of the game were hastily explained to me and as the game progressed, we were joined by a few more children. Some of the older children walked around from the big playground and watched us for a few minutes before they also joined in. Gradually the big playground at the front of the school emptied and the small playground filled as the whole school, including my uncle and Daniel played 'What's The Time, Mr Wolf?'

Since then, I've had thousands of playtimes, but that one remains as the most perfect playtime ever. Though it seems odd that I went to school with my dad's younger brothers and sisters, to have them there and Daniel too, made school even more special. Perhaps Daniel watched out for me because he felt sorry for me. He was a tall and popular blond boy, while I was a shy and quiet brown girl with a scar on my face.

My scar, which lies just underneath my right eye, has an odd and unknown origin. Ask my mother how I got it and her story will go back and forth between: either she doesn't know or I ran into a tray of hot cups of tea. Ask my mother that if I ran into a tray of hot cups of tea so hard that I was left with an indent on my face, why don't I have any burn marks anywhere – then she goes very quiet and changes the subject.

'No one can get a straight answer from my mother about anything, it doesn't even matter what the question is. Even though I grew up playing with my uncles and going to school with them, my mother was weird about them getting close to me and my sisters. We didn't play games which involved physical contact, we only played games like rounders and hide and seek.'

'Ah, that might explain why your uncle Sandeep was standoffish with you at school Jas. Maybe something stemmed from your mother's own childhood that made her wary of things like teenage boys having physical closeness with young girls?'

'I dunno. Who knows what happens in the depths of remote *villages in India. But a lot of things are repeated and reinforced through the generations without anyone really questioning why something's set up the way it is. It's a typical Indian thing though, where there's always a physical distance to be maintained between females and males.'*

'Why the physical distance?'

'There are lots of reasons, most of them stupid, but they all turn on the fact that no family wants a tainted or impure wife for their son. So parents who have daughters will do everything in their power to keep their daughters away from the opposite sex as much as they can so their reputations are as clean and as chaste as possible. Otherwise they believe that no one will want to marry her and they'll be lumbered with her forever.'

'Have you been to India Jas?'

'No, I almost went when I was younger, but instead I ended up going to Birmingham!'

Four

Tea at Amitabh Bachchan's House

'Sit still and don't smile,' instructed my mother.

I grinned before I remembered that I wasn't allowed to smile. Trying not to fall off the high velvet stool, I waited patiently for my photograph to be taken for my passport. I was going to India for three weeks with my parents and my older sister Dimple. Her photograph had been already taken; now it was my turn.

The photographer smiled at me before his face disappeared behind the camera. 'Ok . . . now ready? Just look over here, just here above my head ok?' He patted the top of his head as he bent forward and adjusted the camera lens and then with a bright flash and loud click, my photograph was done.

'Now we can get the forms for your passports sent off,' said my mother as she helped me down. 'There's so much to do before we go and for sure other people will want to give me things to take to their relatives, as if I don't have enough luggage of my own to carry!' My mother huffed, but as she hurried me and Dimple home, one of our white neighbours had given my mother an old second-hand baby walker. After that I stopped crying, happily spending most of the day running around in it.

'There. You play now, ok?' My dad brushed my dark floppy hair out of my eyes and he turned to say goodbye to Mama who was lying on the settee before he left for the pub.

Her arms laden with freshly washed clothes, my mother walked in from the back garden. She glanced around. 'The men have gone already?'

Mama nodded. 'Yes. Tonight's dinner still has to be cooked. The men will want to eat as soon as they return from the pub. You'll have to make roti for them when they get back. Do you want me to help you with anything?'

My mother shook her head. 'You rest, I'll manage.' As my dad relaxed in the pub with the rest of the men, my mother continued on with her daily chores. It was the same every day for my mother, cooking, cleaning, ironing, caring for Mama, looking after her own daughters and my dad's six younger siblings, all while she was pregnant with her fourth child.

After Navi's birth and Mama's subsequent ill health, it was decided that my twenty-one year old dad should get married. Back when my dad had still lived in India, he and my mother had been raised in neighbouring villages and they knew of each other. My dad was considered handsome enough to be a suitable match for my mother who was a year younger. My mother was known for her beauty, while my dad's hard working nature was legendary, not just in his own village, but in the surrounding villages as well.

When he'd been a young boy, my dad had hated going to school. Frequently skipping his lessons, he would head out to the open fields, preferring to help the local villagers on their farms instead. Some of the farmers would keep him for days at a time, until Mama

I could tell that she was excited at the thought of returning to India for the first time since she'd left.

Lost in my daydreams about India, I skipped along the grey pavement. I would meet my young cousins and all of my aunts and uncles. I would run around in big, green fields like I'd seen them do in the Bollywood movies and I'd get to see Amitabh Bachchan, the best actor in the whole wide world.

I turned to my mother. 'Can we go to Amitabh Bachchan's house?'

My mother tutted. 'Don't be silly! He lives in a big city and we're going to our village in the Punjab.'

'But we can go to his house and tell him that we watch all of his films. He will make us some tea if he knows that we've come all the way from England.'

As Dimple tried to stifle her laughter, my mother scoffed. 'Ah yes . . . of course! A big actor like Amitabh Bachchan is going to make you tea because you've come all the way from England! God knows where you get all of your peculiar ideas from! Wait until I tell the rest of the family that you want tea at Amitabh Bachchan's house!'

Falling silent, I consoled myself. Even if I didn't get to see Amitabh Bachchan, I'd still have my cousins to play with.

But several weeks later, I was called into the house by my parents, who told me that I wouldn't be going to India with them and Dimple after all. Instead, while they were in India, me and my younger sister Sarb would stay with my aunt Pupinder in Birmingham and my youngest sisters Pardeep and Bina would go to my aunt Bhav's house in Bentley.

Disappointed and feeling abandoned, tears began to flood my eyes. As I began to sob at the thought of not going to India and of instead being sent to Pupinder's house, I didn't know that my parents could only afford three airline tickets.

Tears rolled down my cheeks. 'But why can't we go to Bhav's house too? Why do me and Sarb have to go to Pupinder's house?'

'Because it'll be too much for your aunt Bhav to have all four of you girls there for three whole weeks. She has to sit and work at her sewing machine all day. Your aunt Pupinder works at her sewing too, but she's got your uncle Manvir to help her. Bhav doesn't get any help from anyone. Her husband Santosh doesn't really help with her sewing work or their three boys. She's got to do everything on her own. We already asked her because we would have preferred to keep all four of you girls together too, but Bhav's already said that she's only willing to take two girls so we've decided that Pardeep and Bina should go to hers. Bhav's house will be better for your younger sisters because Sonny, Baldev and Jaggy will also help look after them,' said my dad.

Sonny, Baldev and Jaggy were Bhav's three sons. For a while, whenever my mother had had a daughter, Bhav had had a son, so her three boys were exactly the same ages as Dimple, me and Sarb. Bhav and her husband Santosh lived behind our house, one house across and the corner of our back gardens joined. Climbing up the branches of the apple tree at the back of our garden, I would call out and chat to my favourite cousins over the garden fence.

Two days after I found out that I wasn't going to India anymore, Sarb and I were driven to Pupinder's house. I had a sinking feeling as the car left the motorway and turned onto the slip-road. When we reached a big roundabout with a crumbling rundown building standing on the middle of it, which my parents used to tell me and my sisters was a witch's house - I knew that we had reached Birmingham. We travelled through narrow streets, passing rows and rows of terrace houses until eventually the car slowed down and then turned left onto a narrow street. The last house, but one in the street belonged to my aunt Pupinder.

My younger cousins had been watching out for us and they flew out of the front door before the car had even come to a standstill. Spilling out onto the pavement, smiling and chatting, they pulled us from the car and into their house.

'Ah, the witches are finally here!'

Recognising the voice, Sarb and I spun around. Standing in the doorway of the kitchen was Pupinder's husband Manvir. It wasn't the first or the last time that he'd refer to me and my sisters as witches.

Wanting to be away from him as quickly as we could, Sarb and I approached our aunt Pupinder as she sat down at her sewing machine. 'Can we play outside?'

Her eyes focused on passing the thread through the eye of the needle, Pupinder nodded. 'Yes, but be careful. Make sure you don't get hurt.'

We slid past Manvir and went out into the garden with our cousins. We were older than our four cousins, Japdeep and her three brothers Hari, Baj and Ishit, but we were wary of them because they didn't play in the same way that we did.

Sarb and I decided to play hop-scotch with Japdeep, but every time we rolled a pebble, her brother Hari would swoop in, pick it up and throw it over the fence and into the neighbour's garden.

I finally lost patience with him as he grabbed another of our pebbles and tossed it over the fence. 'If you do it again Hari, I'm telling!'

My threat fell on deaf ears as Hari threw his head back and laughed, grinning from ear to ear. As Sarb threw another pebble down and prepared to hop, again he scooped it up. As Japdeep and Sarb screeched at him, I ran inside to my aunt.

'Hari isn't letting us play! He keeps on taking our pebble!'

Taking her foot off the pedal of her sewing machine, Pupinder raised her head. 'Tell him I've said that he has to leave you girls alone and let you play.'

I ran back outside to relay his mother's message to him, but to no avail. No sooner had we rolled another pebble, than Hari snatched it up again. This time Sarb and Japdeep both ran inside to tell Pupinder.

'Hari! Come here right now!' Pupinder appeared at the back door, but Hari ignored his mother and ran around the garden instead. With amazing speed for a woman of her size, Pupinder marched up to him and managed to grab him by one of his arms. As Hari kicked and tried to wriggle out of her grasp, she dragged him indoors. Slowly I ambled inside to see Hari get a telling off, but nothing could have prepared me for what happened next.

Pupinder was sitting back down at her sewing machine, but she still had hold of Hari. She kicked and stamped on him and pounded his head and body with clenched fists, not caring where her hits landed. Shocked at this other side to my aunt, I watched silently as Hari tried desperately to free himself from his mother's grip. As his mother's curses, along with kicks and punches rained down on him, screaming and crying he curled up into a ball with his hands around his head. When my aunt finally released him, Hari fled to the furthest corner of the room like a hurt and desperate animal.

Now that I knew what the punishment would be, for the rest of my stay at her house, I never complained to my aunt about any of her children.

Two days before my parents and Dimple were due to return from India, Sarb and I were taken back home to Bentley. Relieved and happy to be home, I relaxed, knowing that I would soon see my parents again.

But as a surprise for my mother, Pupinder and my aunt Pally decided that they would pierce mine and Sarb's ears with a sewing needle that they had sterilized with the flame from the gas cooker. Because I was older than Sarb, I was chosen to go first. I screamed in agony as the hot sewing needle broke through the skin of my ear lobe. But after experiencing such raw pain, I refused to allow them to touch my other ear. Scolding me for my tears, my aunts took hold of Sarb as she gulped, closing her mouth, she screwed her eyes up tightly. But she couldn't keep her mouth closed and was unable to hold in her screams.

By the time my parents returned, my ear was red and swollen with the beginnings of an infection.

'That might help to explain why your cousins turned out the way that they did,' said my therapist.

'Maybe, but I used to get beaten by my mother and I bet there are plenty of other people who got beaten up by their parents and they didn't turn out like my cousins did. Hari ended up dealing drugs and going to prison and Baj beat up his white girlfriend just because she went round to his house, knocked on his front door and asked his mother where he was. While Baj's wife who's from India quietly cooks, cleans and produces grandchildren for his parents!'

'There was a time when I loved my cousins and I would have given my life up for them. But I don't have any sympathy for them anymore, especially after what they did to me. Their mother blames everyone else for her sons' behaviour and as for their father, who used to call me and my sisters witches. While two of his sons went to prison, us witches have university degrees and a couple of us witches have gone on to become founders and owners of successful businesses.'

'I think that goes to the heart of your family, expecting you all to fail because you were girls and yet you have proven, especially you Jas, that being a girl doesn't mean that you won't achieve anything. But weren't your parents upset that some of your relatives would call you witches?'

'Luckily we only had a handful of relatives who thought it was ok to refer to me and my sisters as witches. Occasionally my parents themselves would refer to us as witches, so they weren't particularly upset if they heard someone else calling us witches. When it came to name-

calling, my parents would sometimes call me useless, especially if I didn't get something right the first time around. So from a very young age, I got used to being called a witch and useless. Apart from Dimple, my younger sisters and I were constantly told that we were a burden on our parents and we were a big disappointment for them. We were treated like second-class, always reminded that boys were preferred to girls and that boys should be treated like princes - only Sikh Punjabi boys though, not any other boys.'

Five

By Default

'I'm telling mum when we get home!' Dimple huffed as she stormed off across the playground.

'I don't care!' I shouted at her as she disappeared into the crowd of playing children before I turned and smiled at Jason. 'Come on, let's play tick.'

County Bridge Primary school had finally opened and it was attended by children from all around Bentley. Jason was a year younger than me, but he'd taken to playing with me and my new friends Sally and Sophie.

Later that day when I returned home, my mother called me to her as she stood at the sink, elbow deep in pots and pans.

'Yes mum?' I reached out and tried to catch the bubbles rising up from the washing up soapsuds.

'Jas, you know you're not supposed to talk to boys.'

I stopped trying to catch the bubbles. Of course I knew that my parents didn't want me to talk to boys, but I'd always believed that that was something they just said, not something that they would actually enforce. Gripping the counter edge, I stood up onto my tiptoes as

I tried to look into my mother's face. 'But-' I paused. We weren't allowed to question anything that an adult said to us. On this occasion however, I was unable to stop myself. 'But we play with our cousins all the time and they're boys,' I said. It was true, though in later years, my mother would make no secret of the fact that she didn't like us being close to our male cousins either.

My mother stopped scrubbing and turned to look down at me. 'Sonny and his brothers are different! Don't you remember we've told you all of this before . . . have you forgotten? You're supposed to be a good girl!'

I shook my head. I hadn't forgotten about being a good girl. I let go of the kitchen counter and rested back on my feet.

'Right then,' said my mother. 'Now that I've told you again, don't forget this time. Now go and do your homework. Have you learnt your words yet?'

My teacher typed and then cut out various, different words. She'd place them into old tobacco tins and hand them out to the class to take and learn at home. As soon as I'd learnt my words, my teacher would replace them with new ones. It would take me no time at all to learn the words and loving the lingering smell of long-gone tobacco, I would spill out the pieces of paper onto the carpet and play with the empty tin.

Relieved I wasn't going to completely disappoint my mother. 'I already know all my words,' I said.

Satisfied that she'd put everything back in order, my mother turned her attention back to her pots and pans.

No one in my family or any of the other Sikh Punjabi families that I knew socialised with white people. They didn't want to integrate or try to mix in with anyone outside of the Sikh Punjabi community because they believed that their culture was far superior to that of the English. My family would do whatever they needed to do outside the home - go to school, work, shopping or run errands - but they'd promptly return home and firmly close the door. Since they only talked to outsiders when they needed something from them, it was easy to avoid having any meaningful interaction with anyone outside of our family and community, particularly for family members who didn't have a job outside the home. Most of the women in my family had large industrial sewing machines at home and they were able to work at various sewing jobs without leaving the house.

Confined to the home for the majority of their time, my mother and aunts, like so many of my other female relatives, never bothered to learn to speak English properly. My sisters, cousins and I were fluent in English and Punjabi and during conversations we were all able to move between both languages with ease, sometimes starting a sentence in Punjabi and finishing it in English. If my mother or aunts were ever faced with a white person, they all knew one phrase which they'd pull out with big unassuming smiles and use - 'me no speak English.' Beyond these four words, they didn't feel the need to learn anything else.

At school the next day, I reluctantly explained to Sally and Sophie that I couldn't play with Jason anymore.

'But we were all gonna play tick again!' said Sophie.

'Why? What's he done?' asked Sally. 'Nothin' . . . my mum just said that I'm not allowed to play with boys,' I mumbled.

Confusion and bewilderment mingled on their faces. Sophie and Sally didn't understand, but playtime wasn't to be wasted, so they shrugged and raced off to play. I watched them leave and not knowing what else to do, I sat down on the grassy slope.

Head down, I was trying to make a daisy chain when I heard Jason calling my name.

'Jas! Jas!' He raced up to me. 'Sally and Sophie said . . . they said that you don't wanna play with me anymore?' Panting and out of breath, he held onto his side. 'Come on, let's go. It's a really good game we're playing.'

Abandoning the daisy chain, I got to my feet. 'My mum said I can't play with boys, ok?' I pushed past Jason, knocking him aside as I hurried down the slope towards the school building as signalling the end of playtime, the sound of the bell rang out.

Playtime over, I lined up with my class as my teacher Miss Brown led us back indoors. There was a rumour that Miss Brown kept an old ballet shoe in her desk and she wasn't afraid to use it, but today Miss Brown's shoe was the least of my worries. For the rest of the afternoon, I quietly stewed. Not only had I been mean to Jason, but I'd missed out on having fun with the rest of my friends.

The next day, I felt relieved when Jason left me, Sally and Sophie to play on our own. But at home-time as I was walking towards the school gates with my sisters and my mother, over the babbling stream of other parents and children, we heard a loud voice.

'Excuse me?'

We turned around to see who it was. A white woman stood holding Jason's hand. I immediately knew that this was going to be uncomfortable for my mother. Even if my mother had been able to speak perfect English, she'd never be able to explain why she wouldn't allow her daughters to play with boys.

'I'm Jason's mum. He came home really upset yesterday. I asked him what was wrong and he told me that your daughter said something about how she can't play with him . . . because . . . because he's a boy.' She smiled. 'I'm sure he's just getting mixed up. Sorry, I hope you don't mind me asking, but what exactly did your daughter say to him yesterday?'

I held my breath as I glanced up at my mother. I expected her to fake a big smile, to throw the get-out-of-anything 'me no speak English' line at Jason's mother and apologise for any misunderstanding and that of course I could play with Jason. Instead, my mother looked at Jason's mother for a few moments. Then without a single word or any other form of acknowledgement, she turned around and walked through the school gates, my sisters hurrying alongside her. A few seconds later, I also turned and quietly followed.

Believing that I would be in trouble because Jason's mother had spoken to my mother, I trailed slowly behind my mother and sisters as we made our way home. But from up ahead, my mother stopped and turned around.

She was wearing a big smile. 'Come on, hurry up Jas. You're a good girl, aren't you? See how you listened to me, that's how a good girl should be.'

'I'm just thinking about you being a good girl Jas. And a good student learning all of your words. Were you trying to appease or seek approval from your parents? Or was there something else going on?'

'I don't know if it was appeasement or approval, but I did love studying and reading. I'd read anything and everything that I could get my hands on because books were the only escape I had. I'd be transported into hundreds of fascinating worlds that were different to mine. My family weren't horrible or anything, it's just very restrictive and boring when you're confined to only thinking and doing things that relate to just your own culture and religion.'

'As a young child, I tried not to disappoint my parents - any more than I already had by being born a girl. My birth always weighed heavily on me because my parents, especially my mother made no secret of the fact that having daughters made her life worse and no kid wants to disappoint or add to the troubles of their parents. I think it's a biological thing where kids, especially brown kids have this internal setting, which means they're more susceptible to emotional manipulation and that whole feel-sorry-for-me and don't-even-think-about-disgracing-me thing rammed down their throats from their parents. All of us girls knew that the community and culture was very inward

looking and everyone was always in everyone else's business. Kids were made to feel responsible for maintaining their parents' perfect image and reputation in the community and my parents also played on the fact that they were poor and so already hard-done by in life. Like so many other parents I knew, they used that kind of emotional nonsense to get their kids to do what they wanted them to do and made them feel bad when there was nothing to feel bad about.'

'But what did your parents actually believe was going to happen if they let you talk to boys?'

'Well . . . their thought process was very simple. They thought that talking to a boy may lead to friendship with a boy, which may lead him to becoming a boyfriend, which may lead to sex. That was such a horrifying thought for my parents that it just felt safer for their daughters not to have any friendships with any boys in the first place. By stopping me and my sisters from even talking to boys, by default the ban protected our virginity and helped prevent a shadow from falling over our family's honour.'

'I can't imagine the impact it must have had on you not being allowed to talk to boys. What must that have been like for you Jas?'

'It just became a way of life, a normal state of affairs. Any type of behaviour can be seen as normal if enough people around you are behaving in the exact same way. Because my parents weren't the only ones with these kinds of stupid rules. Most of the brown girls at my school, especially at my secondary school, their parents also had the same rule about them not talking to boys. Imagine if you're the only brown girl who does talk to boys, your behaviour would stick out like a sore thumb and inevitably it would be reported back into the community and give relatives and neighbours a chance to tut-tut and criticise your parents for not raising you properly. But my parents created problems where there didn't need to be any. When you grow up without the freedom to interact with boys outside of your own family, you have no real understanding

or knowledge of the different ways of the wider world. You're not a complete person if you're restricted or prevented from having what is a natural interaction and you don't have the experience of how to interact with boys and it can make them seem to be a bigger deal than what they really are. So even though there are men everywhere in this world and there will continue to be men everywhere in this world, my parents insistence that I ignore boys, meant that boys, especially white boys become almost like aliens, a species that was mysterious. I was taught to disregard people who were different to me - boys and white people. Apart from when we were at school, me and my sisters didn't have any interaction or socialising with anyone outside of our religion and community. We were told that white people had dirty habits, white people didn't understand or care about us. Of course there was always the unspoken worry of experiencing racism and when - not if - it would be inflicted upon us by white people. From watching television and reading newspapers, I knew about skinheads who were always white men, but at school, I did have white girls as friends and so did my sisters. We ignored our family when they'd mutter about white women being trashy.'

'Do you believe that white women are trashy Jas?'

I shook my head. 'No, just like I don't believe that all Indian women are versions of the Goddess Sita.'

Six

Down The Banister

'Mum said we have to get ready! We're going to the gurdwara with Sonny lot!' said Dimple as she rushed around the house, delivering my mother's message.

I put down my book. *Carbonel, the King of Cats* would have to wait. One of the many delights of our house in Bentley was that we lived within walking distance of Willenhall gurdwara.

My mother gathered us by the front door. 'Sonny lot are meeting us at the top of the road so let's hurry up and get going.' Balancing my sister Bina on one of her hips and using her other free hand to grip my sister Pardeep's hand, my mother trusted Dimple, Sarb and I to walk alongside her. With my aunts Pally and Navi tagging along, we all left the house.

My sisters and I were not allowed to wander around to my aunt Bhav's house unless we were invited or accompanying my parents on a visit. We also weren't allowed to go to the local park unless we called on Sonny and his brothers to accompany us.

It was the same with trips to the small library which sat at the bottom of one of the steepest hills in Bentley. I loved going to the library. At first I scarcely believed that I was allowed to read books for free. Ploughing through my library books within a matter of days, I'd then have to wait impatiently for my sisters and cousins to either catch-up or the library books to become due before I was allowed to return and get more books.

As soon as I spotted my favourite cousins waiting restlessly with their mother Bhav at the crossroads, I left my mother's side and raced towards them. The road we had to walk along was busy with traffic, but the pavement was wide. My mother and Bhav ambled along enjoying the outdoors and being away from the demands of the men and housework while with my sisters, cousins, Pally and Navi, I would dart and dash around exploring the gardens and hedges along the way. Sometimes we ran ahead of our mothers and sometimes, if we found something of interest we'd trail behind.

'Come on, let's go down here!' Sonny said as we raced ahead.

Stepping off the pavement, we headed down a grassy incline closely followed by the rest of our siblings to one of our favourite spots. A dry canal, filled in the 1960s, it was overgrown with long blades of green grass, wild flowers and insects. Jumping and laughing, we ran free as we chased each other around. We always stopped at the old canal to explore as much of it as we could, before one of our mothers would inevitably call down. 'Come back up and stop dawdling!'

As we reluctantly climbed back up onto the pavement, our mothers scoffed as they rounded us up.

'How did you manage to get so dirty in such a short time?'

'Look at the state of your hands! Be sure to wash them as soon as you get to the gurdwara!'

As soon as we entered the grounds of Willenhall gurdwara, we immediately became silent and solemn and quickly scrambled to the basket where the headscarves were kept. While our mothers always kept their heads covered with headscarves inside and outside the home, we children only covered our heads while we were in the gurdwara, removing the headscarves and replacing them back into the basket when we were ready to head home.

I took off my shoes and washed my hands. Taking a penny from my mother, I joined my sisters, cousins and aunts as we silently walked in one long trail behind my mother and aunt Bhav into the main prayer hall where the Guru Granth Sahib, the holy scripture was adorned.

Sikhs believe in one God and the Guru Granth Sahib is respected above and beyond any of the ten gurus who founded and stabilised Sikhism in the Punjab. The Guru Granth Sahib had been left by the gurus to ensure that the Sikhs who came afterwards had the divine teachings, guidance and knowledge that they needed to help them achieve a spiritual and meaningful life.

I placed the penny in front of the Guru Granth Sahib and knelt down to the floor, bowing my head. Getting back up, I walked across to my mother and sat down on the floor beside her. I enjoyed the serenity of the gurdwara and listening to the prayers, but as usual I was distracted by one of my cousins.

'Jas! Let's go outside,' whispered Baldev.

I glanced across at my mother. Her eyes half- closed, she was absorbed in the prayers. We were all well-rehearsed at escaping out from under our mothers' watchful gazes. Quietly Baldev and Sarb left first and after they'd both disappeared through the main doors of the prayer hall, I stood up and followed. Leaving one or two at a time, we'd meticulously time our departure so that we usually managed to leave the prayer hall without attracting the attention of our mothers.

'Up here Jas!' hissed Baldev as he stood with Sarb at the top of the long wide staircase.

The staircase led to an upstairs kitchen and a dining hall, but we weren't interested in food. The reason we'd left the prayer hall was to slide down the banister that separated the long wide staircase into two. It was the longest and straightest banister that I'd ever seen.

Children were banned from playing on the stairs, but without any hesitation, I raced up. As I positioned myself carefully across the banister and prepared to let go, Dimple, Sonny and Jaggy came out of the prayer hall and scrambled up the stairs to join us. Letting go, I found myself whizzing all the way down. 'Yah!'

Taking it in turns to slide down, we all knew that no matter how badly or how hard we landed at the bottom, we'd have to quickly get back up onto our feet. The main prayer hall was situated near the foot of the stairs and at any moment any one of the numerous priests could walk out and catch us in mid- whizz or find us sprawled across the floor. There would be no assistance or sympathy, only a sharp clip across the ear. On the odd occasion when one of us had been caught by a priest, the rest of us would magically disperse into the different corners of the gurdwara, leaving the unlucky one to bear the priest's wrath. It was unpleasant to get caught, but the joy of sliding down the banister far outweighed the risk of a roasting.

The gurdwara was huge, full of nooks and crannies it made for an ideal play area, especially for games like hide and seek. We rarely got caught because most of our mischief was done ever so quietly and we weren't destructive or rowdy either. As I grew older, my sisters and I were expected to help in the gurdwara kitchen, working under the guidance of other older women to help cook and prepare food for the congregation. Most of the other women who served in the kitchen were nice to us, but some would begrudge our presence, insisting that only they could do the job well, but service in a gurdwara is open to anyone who wants to do it. And on several occasions when my family would hold a celebration at the gurdwara and we had to take full responsibility for the entire kitchen's work, my mother and aunts would politely, but firmly shoo those women into one corner.

'It sounds as if your culture was preparing you and your sisters for stereotypical female roles Jas. Your male cousins didn't help out in the kitchen of the gurdwara?'

'No, not at first. Serving in a kitchen wasn't really considered to be a boy's job, but Sonny lot wanted to be where me and my sisters were because they'd get bored playing on their own. So they used to kick up a fuss and eventually, much to the disapproval of the other women, my mother would let the three boys into the kitchen. But if the boys didn't want to help, they didn't have to, whereas us girls always had to be in the kitchen. When the boys helped out, they were treated as if they were doing something special and deserved praise, but with us girls, the attitude was . . . oh well, that's what a girl's supposed to do. And even though Sikh men and Sikh women are equal in the eyes of God, funnily enough after the women had done most of the hard graft in the kitchen, cooking for several hours, the men would swoop in and take over the ceremonial part of serving the prepared food to the Guru Granth Sahib. Men always seem to take the most important and visual part of any ceremony, especially a religious one because clearly it's not just about serving God, it's about being seen to serve God.'

'Yet despite all the obvious inequality that surrounded you Jas, you still somehow managed to carve out some happy moments.'

I smiled. 'My early childhood in Bentley was far from perfect, but it was happy. Between Willenhall gurdwara, the local park, the library, the swing that the adults had put up for us kids in the garden, the apple tree and the fields and the meadows around Bentley, I spent most of my earlier childhood running around with my sisters, cousins, aunts and uncles. One time, my uncle Taran took us all out on an adventure. We started exploring a meadow by our local park and somehow ended up walking along the M6! Following my uncle in a straight line, we walked for several miles along the motorway and when we returned home, we never breathed a word to our parents. Some of my fondest memories as a child are of me playing with my cousins in the gurdwara. We weren't loud or rowdy, so we didn't really draw attention to ourselves. Being children, we did the usual pushing and shoving because we weren't perfect, but unlike my cousins from Birmingham, we weren't aggressive or destructive.'

Seven

Why Blame A Boy

'They're here!'

At the sound of Sarb's voice, I lifted my head and glanced up. I had been playing with a small anthill at the bottom of the garden, letting the ants run up and down my arm, humming softly to myself. Sensing my grandmother's presence next to me, I had become still. Mama did not visit often, but when she did, knowing that she never stayed long, I always made sure to savor the moment.

Now that moment had been abruptly broken as my uncle Sandeep pulled into the driveway with Pupinder, Manvir and my four cousins. As the children tumbled out of the car, I learnt from their excited chatter that they would be staying for the whole weekend.

'What're you doing?' Ishit wandered over to where I was crouching.

'Nothing.' I shrugged as I got to my feet. I towered over my younger cousin as I straightened up. I tried to appear nonchalant and hoped that he wouldn't notice the ants, but he'd already spotted them.

'Ants! Let me look!'

I stepped aside as Ishit knelt down next to the anthill. I watched silently as he picked up a small twig from the ground and began to poke and prod at the ants. Grinning he looked up at me. 'I'm gonna get some water and watch 'em swim!'

'Don't be stupid Ishit! Ants can't swim!'

Chuckling he jumped to his feet. 'So?' Brushing past me, he raced inside. A few minutes later, clutching a glass of water, he emerged from the back door.

'Don't Ishit!' I said. 'Here, I'll show you how you're supposed to play with 'em . . . we can play together.'

But Ishit tightened his grip around the glass and in one swoop emptied the entire contents onto the anthill. It collapsed, becoming soggy and mud-like. Some of the ants fled underground, but many more floated lifeless in the slush. Not content, Ishit began to stamp on what remained of the anthill. 'Stupid ants! Look at 'em swim!' His feet demolished what the water had spared and the anthill was almost completely destroyed. Ishit laughed. 'See! See what I done!'

I could see. Furious I slapped him across his face. As his gleeful expression turned to one of shock, I pushed him down onto the soggy ground he'd made. His wailing interrupted the play of the other children who gathered around as our mothers hurried outside.

'Jas, did you hit your cousin?' asked my mother. 'Yeah . . . only cos he killed all the-'

'You know you're not supposed to hit your cousin! You're so useless!' My mother lunged forward. Grabbing my arm she swung me around and gave me two hard slaps on my back. 'He's smaller than you! If you hit him again, you're going to get properly beaten. Do you understand?'

As soon as my mother let me go, I retreated upstairs to the girls' bedroom, bruised and annoyed that despite what he'd done, Ishit was getting all the sympathy.

The following morning, my grandfather got ready to go to his garden allotment. The local council had given him a spacious plot directly behind the row of houses opposite our house and he would spend a lot of time there growing fruit and vegetables.

My sisters and I along with Sonny, Baldev, Jaggy loved going to the allotment and as long as we didn't speak to my grandfather or disturb him while he was planting, he didn't grumble too much if we tagged along.

At first the other allotment owners were worried by the sight of so many young children running around between their small plots of land, but we'd proven to them that despite our numbers and the speed at which we could run, we could be trusted not to trample over their fruit and vegetables. Slowly the other owners had become used to seeing us, sometimes sharing the fruits of their labour with us.

'Can I go to the allotment?' I asked my dad. 'Please . . . I'll be good.'

My dad nodded as my cousins Hari and Baj also piped in. 'We wanna go as well!'

Clutching a small plastic bag containing the new seeds that he intended to plant, my grandfather looked down at his grandchildren with a heavy face.

He sighed. 'Alright. As long as you all behave, I don't want any mischief.'

Promising faithfully to be good, we started on the short journey to the allotment walking behind my grandfather. Crossing over the road, down the alleyway and around the back of the houses and pushing open the heavy metal gate to the allotment. It was empty, none of the other allotment owners were there.

But no sooner had the gate closed behind us, than Hari and Baj scattered in different directions as if they'd suddenly been released from a cage. Throwing up dirt and soil under their feet, it took them only a few minutes before they'd trodden over most of the plots. Plants and vegetation lay flattened and in disarray. It would have been impossible to catch them in the open space. Anger and disappointment was etched on my grandfather's red face as he stood on the gravel path, shouting helplessly at them to stop.

Standing next to my grandfather, I watched silently. I couldn't understand my cousins' behavior and just as I thought things couldn't get any worse, at the sudden loud squeak of the metal gate, I spun around to see two of the other allotment owners walk through to bear witness to the carnage.

'Jas, I'm just wondering where your anger went when your cousin destroyed the anthill? It couldn't have been easy to stand there and watch all those ants die.'

'From a very young age, I was told that my feelings and thoughts were not important. I had been taught that I was never to show my emotions and I had to hold everything in because nobody was going to listen or give a shit, so my anger didn't really have anywhere to go. Though on this occasion, I whacked Ishit so some of my anger did come out!'

'I get the sense from what you describe of your family that boys could never be blamed or criticised?'

I nodded. 'Yes . . . why blame a boy if there's a girl around to take the fall? My grandfather used the allotment incident as an excuse not to take us girls down there anymore either. If it really had been any of us girls who did the damage, my grandfather probably would have battered us. In my house, any adult could smack any child and no one would even bat an eyelid. My mother would give me a smack across the head and back and on the odd occasion I'd get a proper beating from her. I'd get thumped and slapped, but the worst beating I ever got was from my uncle Taran.'

Eight

They Knew And I Knew

'Now listen up children! You're not to give your aunt Harjit any trouble or disturb her while she's working, do you understand?' said my mother.

My uncle Manjeet had recently married a girl called Harjit from India. While the rest of my family and my parents were going to visit my aunt Pupinder, my new aunt had decided to stay at home. Not wanting to be dragged to Birmingham and using the advantage of having an adult stay behind who could supervise us, Dimple, Sonny and I begged our mothers to allow us to remain home.

'It's the first time Harjit's going to be left on her own with you children, so all three of you better behave,' warned my mother.

We all nodded earnestly.

As the rest of the family left and the house became quiet, I headed upstairs to the girls' bedroom and curling up on one of the bunk beds, I was soon caught up in the mischievous tales of *My Naughty Little Sister*. I was so engrossed that a little while later when Dimple and

Sonny stuck their heads around the door, I barely glanced up.

'Do you wanna come and play with us Jas?' asked Sonny.

I shook my head. 'No, I'm reading.'

'Come on . . . we're going to play with uncle Taran's train set,' said Dimple.

Frowning I raised my head. On the first day that he'd brought his prized train set home, my uncle Taran had given a warning to everyone that it wasn't to be touched. 'But uncle Taran said we ain't allowed to play with his train set!'

'Oh shut up!' said Dimple.

'You can stay here if you want, but we're gonna play with it,' said Sonny as he grinned.

They disappeared, closing the door behind them.

I shrugged. Surely Dimple and Sonny weren't really going to disobey such strict orders. I turned back to my book and was completely lost in the tales of Shirley Hughes when the sound of an angry voice from downstairs drifted up and started to pull me away from the pages. As I listened, I realised that it was my uncle Taran's voice and he sounded furious.

As I continued to listen, I heard a loud pounding. Someone was stomping up the stairs. Suddenly the bedroom door was flung open and my uncle Taran was standing over me. He looked angrier than I'd ever seen him look before.

'Get downstairs! Right now!' he shouted.

I quickly put my book down and I scrambled off the bed and onto my feet. With my uncle on my heels, I hurried downstairs. I turned into the living room as my aunt Harjit, who was standing inside the kitchen, firmly closed the kitchen door, shutting herself away from whatever was about to unfold.

Dimple and Sonny were already standing in the living room, looking as if they were about to cry. I knew instantly that something had happened with Taran's train set, but I wasn't worried. Whatever it was, I knew that it hadn't been me.

My uncle Taran ordered the three of us to stand in a line and anxious not to invoke more of his anger, we quickly lined up.

'Who touched my train set? It's broken! I want to know who touched it?' Taran began shouting in our faces.

I glanced sideways at Dimple and Sonny, expecting my sister and cousin to own up, but to my shock they both remained silent.

'You were all told never to touch my train set and now it's broken! Who touched it? Who broke it?' Red with fury, Taran began marching up and down in front of us like a disappointed army general.

Unfortunately I found his marching so comical that, unable to stop myself, I burst out laughing.

'You!'

Before I could say or do anything, my uncle grabbed me by the scruff of my neck and as Dimple and Sonny silently watched on, Taran slapped and punched me, hitting me again and again.

I was helpless to defend myself against my uncle and it was only after he'd released me, blind with tears and pain that I managed to stumble out of the living room and up to the girls' bedroom. Collapsing onto one of the beds, my head was spinning and my chest was pounding so hard that I could barely breathe as I struggled to control my deep raking sobs. My face and body felt as if they were on fire as they began to swell, red, black and blue.

'Jas?' My aunt Harjit had come upstairs to check on me.

I heard the sound of my dad's Beetle pulling into the driveway. As Harjit hurried downstairs to my parents, I started to drift off into a pain-induced sleep.

'Jas?'

Barely able to open my swollen eyes, I saw both my parents standing over me.

'Your uncle hit you?'

'He hit me a lot,' I mumbled. Full of pain, I closed my eyes and drifted into sleep.

My parents never cared who disciplined me and my sisters, we were open to being shouted at or having a clip around the ear or worse from anyone, but this was different. There was a huge argument about the severity of the beating and because my parents didn't want to be questioned by my teachers, I was kept off school for weeks until the bruising had gone down.

'And what was Sonny and Dimple's punishment?' asked my therapist.

'They didn't have a punishment because I never told on them. I thought that they'd own up so I wouldn't have to rat them out, but they never did. Everyone, including my parents, thought that I'd broken my uncle's train set. Dimple and Sonny didn't know right from wrong because they just stood there quietly and let me take the blame for something that they'd done.'

'And to take the blame for something that you haven't done, isn't that wrong?'

'I never really thought of it like that before. I was wrong to take the blame for something that I didn't do. When I was growing up, I didn't stick up for myself much. I used to stay quiet even in the face of accusations and sometimes my silence would be taken as an acknowledgment of my alleged guilt when I hadn't even done anything. I never even confronted Dimple and Sonny about the broken train set, but they knew and I knew what they'd done. I always thought that the oldest protected the youngest because I was like that with my younger sisters, Sarb, Pardeep and Bina, but Dimple didn't protect me. Quite the opposite.'

Nine

Never Outright

'Owwww!' In excruciating pain, I howled at the top of my lungs. Then just as suddenly as I had started to scream, I went mute and watched in horror as the front of my t-shirt turned bright red.

Still recovering from the train set incident, I had ventured outside. But as I stood and watched my sisters and cousins playing a game of catch, Dimple had quickly walked across to me and without any warning, slammed the ball into my face as hard as she could. I heard the loud crack of my bone as the ball smashed into the bridge of my nose.

At the sound of my cries, the adults rushed out of the house. My mother reached me first. She immediately put out one arm to steady me and as my dad and uncle Manjeet gathered around, small pieces of red flesh began falling out of my nose and mixing with the puddle of blood on the ground.

'What happened?' My mother did not bat an eyelid if I fell out of a tree, slipped off the roof of the garden shed or fell into a bush of nettles, but her eyes were panicked when she saw blood and flesh forming a pool at my feet.

'Dimple hit the ball in my face!' I wailed as I swayed on my feet. 'She did it on purpose.'

'Dimple!' My mother tutted at my sister, before she turned back to me. 'Why were you even standing over here? Didn't I tell you to be careful if you were going to play outside?'

'You can tell Jas off afterwards, let's just get her inside first,' said my uncle Manjeet. 'Come on Ugly Duckling.' And with that my uncle picked me up and carried me into the house. As blood continued to pour out of my nose, the front of his favourite blue shirt turned red.

'No one even told Dimple off. Instead I got blamed for standing in the wrong place, even though she'd crossed over to where I was and smacked the ball right into my face.'

'Why do you think she did that?'

'Because she could never outright tell me that she didn't like me.'

'Why do you think she disliked you?'

'I dunno . . . I never did anything to her. Maybe it's because I learnt to read before she did. We were in the same class in 'the cowsheds' school before County Bridge opened and I'd learnt all of my homework words and Dimple was called up by our teacher straight after me, but she didn't know some of her words. I think that was partly because when she'd got back from India with my parents, she'd been ill and had time off school, but also she wasn't really into schoolwork. But our teacher had pointed out that her younger sister had learnt all her words and she hadn't, so maybe she felt that I'd shown her up.'

'Dimple was the eldest daughter and the oldest grandchild and my parents were adamant that as first in line, she had to get everything and do everything first. My parents expected the rest of us to file behind Dimple, we were like an afterthought. That was how Dimple saw it as

well - she knew her place and we should know ours, but unwittingly I didn't obey the line. I just plodded along at my own pace, but I could run faster, climb trees higher and I was good at academic studies so I overtook Dimple. We both excelled at cooking and cleaning because we'd been made to do all of that stuff from a young age, but everything else about us was very different.'

Ten

A Child Like Her

'Hurry up,' said my mother.

Not recognising the part of Wolverhampton that she'd brought me to, I struggled to keep up as we rushed along narrow streets lined with terrace houses. With her head down, my mother scurried along the pavement. Passing house after house, eventually she came to a stop at a front door that looked exactly the same as all the others on the street.

Hesitating, she glanced up and down the deserted and empty street before raising her hand and knocking on the front door.

The door swung open almost immediately. Curious I peered around my mother to see whose house we'd arrived at, but I couldn't see anything beyond the dusty gloom filling the front room.

'I-is the b-baba here?' asked my mother. 'One of my neighbours . . . Saranjit told me he lives here . . . is this the right house?'

I bristled. Now I understood why my mother had lied. She'd told my dad that she was taking me to a doctor's appointment, but instead she'd brought me to see a baba. Babas are men and occasionally women, who pretend that they possess special powers and practice black magic, claiming they're able to cure everything from relationship problems to cancer. Unfortunately their practices were widespread and accepted within the Sikh Punjabi and the wider Indian community and used and funded especially by women. My dad strongly disapproved of babas, hating the mere mention of them. According to him, they were all fraudsters who blandly ripped off uneducated and superstitious people who didn't know any better.

Having been taught about superstitious rituals and customs from a young age, they were a part of my daily life; if someone happened to sneeze as they were preparing to leave the house, they wouldn't be allowed to leave for a few minutes because a sneeze just prior to leaving was considered to be a bad omen for a journey. A sneeze at any other time meant that someone was thinking of you.

Stepping over someone who was sitting or lying down on the floor meant that they would stop growing unless the action was immediately reversed by stepping back over them again.

Upon the birth of a new baby, especially if it was a boy, all visitors had to eat some sugar before they were allowed near the baby in case an evil spirit had attached itself to them during their journey. Eating something sweet like sugar was thought to ward off evil spirits and protect the baby.

My sisters and I were not allowed to wash our hair on certain days of the week because it might bring bad luck. If we'd had a brother, then there would have been other specific days that we'd have to avoid washing our hair to prevent bad luck or death happening to our brother. We'd also get an immediate roasting from my mother if any of us took our shoes off and left them lying upside down with the sole facing up.

This kind of superstitious nonsense was a part of everyday occurrence observed by all the Sikh Punjabi families that I knew, but babas were in a more sinister league.

'Ah yes, come in. I've been expecting you. Come in sister,' said a low quiet male voice from behind the front door.

My mother quickly stepped inside, dragging me along with her. No sooner had we stepped inside than the front door was closed behind us.

'This way sister.' A tall thin Indian man led us through the front room and into a dark living room.

Two young girls were playing on the floor and from behind a closed door, I could hear the sound of running water and the muffled clang of pots and pans.

'Sit down,' said the man as he sank down onto one of the two settees in the room.

Smiling nervously, my mother perched herself on the edge of the other settee. I crouched down onto the floor and joined the two girls as they played, but the man began to frown as he stared at me. Just as I started to feel uneasy under his piercing glare, he called out in a brisk voice making me jump and my mother shuffle uncomfortably.

'Listen here! Come and get the girls!'

Abruptly the sounds of running water and clanging pots stopped and a woman bustled in. She didn't pause in her stride and ignoring both me and my mother, she quickly gathered up the two girls and herded them out of the room. With no one left to play with, I stood up and joined my mother on the settee.

'Sister, you can't bring a child like her into my house without warning me first.' He leaned forward. 'I don't want anything to influence my two daughters.'

As my mother started to apologise, the man waved one of his hands at her, dismissing her. 'I can tell you that she's got a curse, I recognized that right away. Have you thought about what you're going to do about it?'

My mother gave a nervous laugh. 'Well . . . I don't know anything about these sorts of things. I said that to Saranjit as well when she told me about you. I thought I'd come and see what you tell me to do because even if I knew what to do, my husband won't let me try anything. He doesn't believe. You know how some men are about this kind of thing. Even today, I've come here without telling him, he'd be very angry if he found out.'

The man nodded as he sat back. 'And have you thought about her future if you do nothing?'

'Perhaps you can suggest something,' said my mother. 'Her grandmother remains around her. This kind of thing happens in my husband's family and we don't really think too much about it. It goes back to my husband's ancestors. Outside of the family, we don't mention it to anyone.'

The man raised his eyebrows. 'In that case, I can't do anything, it might backfire on me. The only thing I can think of is a group of babas in India who I know. They may help if you take her-'

'But her father will never agree to send her to India!'

The man got to his feet. 'Then there's nothing else I can suggest. I can't do anything myself, but if you change your mind about India, then come back here anytime.'

Standing up, my mother began to rummage around in her bag. She pulled something out and handed it to the man who accepted it without a word. Then he ushered us out of his house and firmly closed his front door.

As she hurried me home, my mother turned to me. 'You missed out on our last trip to India, but maybe you should go on the next one.'

I shrugged as I struggled to keep up with her. 'I've got to return my library books, so I can't go to India.'

'Anytime anyone goes to a baba, they'll be told that they've got a curse. This kind of nonsense is rife in India, but if you

tell a white person that there's black magic being practiced in abundance right here, right now in the UK, they won't believe you. I've heard the stories and dragged along by my mother, I've encountered a few babas myself. They behave like Gods and unfortunately dumb people treat them as if they really are Gods. Naturally, these babas manage to make a lot of money. They thrive because of people's willingness, usually women's willingness, to blindly believe what they're told.'

'The most horrific story I heard was about this Indian woman. She may have been in England, but I'm not really sure . . . anyway she couldn't have any children. Some women can't and that's just how life is, but she was told by some asshole baba that in order to get pregnant, she'd need to eat someone else's child. So she pretended that she was a babysitter and she took someone's baby and began to cook it so she could eat it. The mother of this child turned up and managed to stop her from eating it, but by then the baby was already dead. That's an extreme example, but there are probably hundreds more stories like that about stupid people doing stupid things.'

'But you protected your mother and you didn't tell your dad about the visit?'

'I didn't tell anybody. My dad would have ripped my mother to shreds. Apart from Amritsar, you know where the 'Golden Temple' is? It's the holiest place in the world for Sikhs, the only other place that my dad accepts as blessed is a shrine in the Punjab in India which is known for being very powerful. It used to belong to a devotee of the Prophet Mohamed. After India was divided and Pakistan was created, this devotee left and moved to Pakistan. My mother's family moved from Pakistan to the Punjab and they took over responsibility as caretakers for this place. They don't have mumbo-jumbo stuff going on down there and certainly none of this black magic stuff. Local villagers and the general public are all welcome there. Sikhs, Hindus and Muslims all come to pay their respects. That's the kind of magic that is truly amazing because it unites people of

all religions and backgrounds . . . though sometimes it seems as if nothing can unite people, not even having the same blood.'

Eleven

The Same Every Friday

'You've filled my house with girls! Five of them! How are you going to manage this spare burden that you've created?' My grandfather shouted as he slammed his fist down onto the coffee table. At the sight of my grandfather snarling and with the sound of his fist hitting the coffee table ringing in my ears, I scurried upstairs to the safety of the girls' bedroom.

Every Friday, my dad would be paid for his work at the foundry and he would hand over the brown envelope containing his entire week's wages to my grandfather.

As he shoved the envelope into his trouser pocket, my grandfather's response would be to shout at my dad. It was the same every Friday. 'You're going to end up on the streets! Do you hear me?! I'm going to kick you and your five daughters out! You'll end up on the streets with them! Begging for food! That's what happens when you have five daughters. All of you will amount to nothing!'

Listening in silence, my dad never answered him back. Sometimes he would clear his throat as if he were about to speak, but he never did.

Huddled in the bedroom with my sisters, I listened in wide-eyed silence as my mother recalled a horrid tale. 'It's rumoured that your grandfather killed one of his daughters and there have been others that people say he drowned as soon as they were born.'

Back when my grandparents had still lived in India, Mama had given birth to a girl. Furious and disappointed, my grandfather attempted to leave his newborn daughter on the steps of the local gurdwara. The priest tried to stop him and an argument broke out between the two men, with the priest begging my grandfather not to abandon the child. Eventually, but reluctantly my grandfather had picked up the newborn and taken her back home – she had died nine days later.

I could easily see my grandfather drowning his daughters. He had never shown me or my sisters any love or affection. All of our relatives could see how he treated my parents and us girls, our relatives were sympathetic, especially since my dad never answered or argued back.

But the fact that my dad quietly took all of the insults and degrading comments from my grandfather, ignited an inkling in me that maybe there was some truth in what my grandfather was saying. That maybe as a girl, I really was a spare burden. I had been taught from a very young age, having already committed a serious error by being born a girl, that the very least I could do for my poor parents was not to add to their troubles, to behave responsibly and fulfil their every wish. I was taught that I should always think about others first and that other peoples' wants and wishes were more important than anything I could want or wish.

My mother sighed. 'No one wants girls born into their family, but it would be my bad kismet that all the girls that your grandfather killed in India have been reborn in my house as the five of you! You've all been reborn from the daughters he drowned and now your poor father has to hear about it!'

'It's considered normal in lots of Sikh Punjabi families for a son to hand over all of his wages to his parents every week, every month of every year. If he's handing over his wages to his parents for years and years, he'll never be in a position to buy his own home and separate from them. All he can do is hold out hope for inheritance after his parents die. He's financially tied into remaining with them and looking after them into their old age - though the reality is that it's actually the poor daughter-in-law who'll end up looking after her husband's parents until they die.'

'It's about keeping control over your children. So even though they may be financially supporting the household, sons remain childlike because they're never really independent or given any real responsibility. Decisions are usually made by their parents and the adult sons will accept those decisions and expect their wives to quietly follow - ideally several feet behind!'

'And what about daughters Jas?'

'Daughters aren't considered to be of any financial benefit to parents. They don't see a daughter as a wage earner or see any benefit in letting her further her education so she can get a job. Daughters are considered to be a liability so the family will try and marry her off as soon as they can. They think that if a girl doesn't get married off at a young age and she goes off to university, she'll have freedom away from her family and community. She may sleep with lots of boys, even one boy would be too many for most families and no would-be-in-laws want a non-virgin as a wife for their son. A daughter can also bring the family's honour into disrepute by sleeping around and fall pregnant so early marriage is there to keep girls away from sexual exploits.'

'How did it make you feel to know that your parents would have preferred to have had boys? Because a first

born girl can be forgiven, because it's the first child, but then to have a second child who is also a girl? That couldn't have been so easy for your parents to accept . . . as far as they were concerned, you should have been a boy.'

'Well, I wasn't a boy. My mother always said that if I'd been a boy, she wouldn't have had any more children. That made me feel even more unwanted and useless. Just by being born I'd already disappointed my parents and probably other people in the house as well. Apart from my aunt Navi, none of my dad's family really showed any affection towards me and my sisters. While my grandfather's anger was voiced loudly, some of my dad's brothers and sisters had a quiet indifference towards us. I remember when Sonny lot would visit us, Pally would cook special treats and food for them, which my sisters and I weren't allowed to have.'

'Usually the eldest son is given the most respect, but my grandfather was angry that my dad had five daughters and he was also giddy on the fact that he had three other sons living with him. I dunno if I really believe in karma and all that stuff, but I do think that the sound of my grandfather's fist hitting the coffee table every Friday, that thud was heard somewhere in the remote corner of the universe that deals with karma.'

Twelve

That Old Beetle!

'Girls come on . . . let's go.' My mother ushered me and my sisters into the back seat of my dad's old Beetle.

When my grandfather's shouting became too much, my parents would bundle me and my sisters into the car and we'd drive out into the countryside. The farther the car travelled from my grandfather's temper, the happier my parents became. Living with a large extended family, our little trips to the countryside were a rare opportunity for me and my sisters to spend time alone with my parents.

These drives were one of the few times that I felt my parents were relaxed and cared about us. Usually they had very little, if any, time for us. My dad would be at work all day and my mother would be in the kitchen or busy with other household chores. Unless we were in trouble, the only time we'd get any attention from either parent would be if and when they needed us to do something for them, like fetch something from the kitchen or from upstairs.

For a while when my dad had worked the early morning shift at the foundry, I had taken to waking up at the crack of dawn and sneaking downstairs to spend a few minutes alone with him as he got ready to leave. While my dad believed I'd wake up early just to have some of the tea he made and though I loved drinking tea, it wasn't the tea that got me out of bed while it was still dark outside. In the quiet of the kitchen, even if it was only for a few scarce minutes, I relished being alone with my dad. Watching him quietly and steadily pour two cups of tea, the serenity of those moments would carry me through the rest of the day.

Once a year, we would visit Blackpool, Drayton Manor or West Midlands Safari Park with the rest of our forty-plus family. For the trips to the theme parks, my mother and my aunts would wake up at 5am and cook parathas, make sandwiches, pile pickles into containers and pour tea into numerous flasks. Leaving the sandwiches until later, we'd tuck into the parathas as soon as we reached our destination, ignoring the curious glances from the white people strolling past in the car park. Even cold, the parathas tasted delicious.

The little trips we took to the countryside just on our own were the only times my mother got any respite from the never-ending drudgery of housework, while my dad simply relished any opportunity he got to drive his beloved Beetle.

Though we all loved the Beetle, the only thing predictable about the car was that during any given journey, at some point it would break down. My dad couldn't afford to have breakdown cover, so regardless of wind, rain or the bemused looks from other drivers who'd have to manoeuvre around us, all of us would have to pile out and push the broken down car to safety.

'Dad, can we stop and look at that horse in that field?'

As my dad drove us deeper into the countryside, I spotted a black horse standing alone at the far end of a large field. Horses were my favourite animal and I couldn't help, but ask.

My dad glanced over at the horse and then asked my mother if he should stop. My mother nodded and my dad pulled over to the side of the quiet road. The Beetle was a two-door car and my mother had to get out of the passenger seat first and pull the backrest forward so my sisters and I could all exit.

'Cross the road carefully now,' my mother said as one by one, we scrambled out of the car.

I was first across the road and I stopped by the fence. The horse standing on the far side of the field, lifted his head and looked towards us. His neck arched up and his head was raised high and he stood very still.

I turned and beckoned to my sisters. 'Look how beautiful he is! He's amazing, isn't he?'

As Dimple loitered by the car, Sarb and Pardeep hurried across the road to join me at the fence.

'He's coming over here,' exclaimed Pardeep.

I turned back round to look at the horse. It had started a leisurely saunter across the field towards us, but as I watched, it broke into a gallop and within a few seconds he was bolting, heading straight for the fence where I was standing with my sisters.

My dad was about to get out of the driver's seat and join us when I turned and called over my shoulder. 'There's summat wrong with the horse!'

My mother took a brief glance at the horse and realised that something was very wrong with it.

'Come back over here! Quickly! Hurry! Get back in the car before he gets here and jumps over the fence!'

With Sarb and Pardeep, I raced back across the road. My dad began to turn the ignition key as my mother frantically threw us onto the back seat of the car. We landed on top of one another, but we were so petrified by the horse that we didn't care about being hit by knees and elbows.

'Hurry up and start the car!' My mother screeched, jumping into the passenger seat she quickly slammed her door shut. 'Let's get out of here!'

'I'm trying!' Frantically, my dad tried to start the Beetle. 'Come on! Come on!' Even above our screeching, all we could heard was the sound of a dull lifeless click as the Beetle refused to start.

Every time my dad desperately turned the ignition key, he also turned his head to see how close the horse was. It was approaching so quickly that my dad made no attempt to be calm. 'Come on! Start! Start!'

The horse had almost reached the fence and it was clear that there was no way that it was going to contain his speed and force. In unison, we all shrieked, believing that the horse was going to jump over the fence and land on our car, when with a sudden roar the Beetle suddenly sprung to life. In an instant my dad had pulled away from the field. As we whizzed past, the horse came to an abrupt stop at the fence, his head reared up, his wide eyes seemed crazed and he was stamping his feet.

As the Beetle sped down the road, we fell back into our seats. Filled with relief that we'd left the crazy horse behind, we all burst into laughter.

From the passenger seat, my mother laughed. 'We'll never do that again! What a crazy horse! I thought for sure that we were all going to die today!'

'Jas . . . I think from now on, you should only look at horses in books or from far away when we drive past them in our car,' said my dad as he drove us back home.

It was perhaps the only time in my life that I was inclined to agree wholeheartedly with my parents.

'Years later my dad sold the Beetle and bought a second hand Ford Sierra. On the very first day we got our new car, we were all so excited and we begged my dad to take us for a ride around the streets. We were so glad to see the back of that old Beetle! I remember feeling very smug that unlike the Beetle, the Sierra would never break down. But my dad

hadn't checked the fuel gauge after he'd collected the car from the sales guy and unbelievably on its maiden journey, the Sierra ran out of petrol and stopped. So then we all had to get out and push it to the nearest petrol station which of course was miles away and I wasn't feeling so smug anymore! It's funny because we loved the Ford Sierra, but it's always the old Beetle that we still talk about.'

'Maybe because the Beetle connects you to the happier times you shared with your parents Jas.'

'Yeah, it did. My parents weren't completely psychotic. When we went to theme parks with the rest of our family, my parents would let me and my sisters wander around without any supervision, but some of my female cousins and my aunts Pally and Navi had to remain with the adults. They weren't allowed to wander off on their own like we were.'

'What did the adults think was going to happen at these theme parks?'

'Who knows?! Maybe between riding the rollercoaster and the pirate ship, one of my female relatives might meet someone and lose her virginity. Some of the men in my family were obsessed with controlling the women. I don't think it's very complicated - most problems in a lot of Sikh Punjabi families can be traced back to control, who wants it and who can enforce it onto other family members. The men in my family exercised control over the women so the women lived the life that the men wanted them to live. Here's the thing though, the men made sure that the women knew that they were being watched. Knowing that you're constantly being watched and your behaviour is being monitored and judged, is stifling and this monitoring was deliberately done openly so the women would keep themselves in check rather than face punishment from the men. Sometimes male control is subtle and sometimes it's not, but the end result is always the same...continued misery for the woman if she stays in that environment.'

Thirteen

My Grandfather's Daughter

'We're moving so you'll have to return all of your library books,' said my mother.

I lifted my eyes from the pages of *Ramona The Pest*. 'We're moving out?'

My mother nodded. 'Your dad and I have bought a house in Walsall. It's only five minutes from here. It's right next door to a hospital, it's close to the town and market and there are schools nearby for all you girls.'

I had never heard of Walsall, but I didn't need to ask my mother why we were moving - I had already heard my grandfather telling my parents to get out before he kicked them out. None of my dad's brothers or sisters said anything, they just watched silently. No one even stated the obvious, that out of my grandfather's four sons, my dad had contributed the most financially to the household.

It would take an outsider, Bhav's brother-in-law Guneet to step in and help my parents. He knew that my parents had no money, but in their time of need, Guneet had struck a deal with them. Guneet and his family would move out of their three-bed terrace house in Walsall and my parents would move in. They would pay him whenever and whatever they could afford until the purchase price of eleven thousand pounds was all paid off. And while Guneet and his family looked for a new home for themselves, they would stay with Guneet's brother Ram, who lived next-door to our new house.

It was not unusual for members of Sikh Punjabi families, especially brothers to live next door to each other or in the same street.

A few days before our move, I heard something that I'd never heard before or ever again since - my mother arguing with my grandfather.

'I've raised her as one of my own since Mama died. You'll have no more worry or burden of her if you let her come with us,' said my mother. 'We'll look after her as if she was one of our own daughters.'

'Navi's going to stay here with me and the rest of her family and that is final. I'll have no more discussion about it,' stated my grandfather.

My mother began to sob as my dad tried to convince my grandfather to let Navi live with us, but it was no use.

My grandfather was adamant. 'Have you forgotten that you're not Navi's only brother? She has other brothers who'll still be here in this house after you've gone!'

As our moving day inched closer, Navi's sadness was tangible, but there was nothing my parents could do. She was my dad's youngest sister and my mother had raised her since she was a toddler, but she was still my grandfather's daughter.

For the last evening in my childhood home and as a treat for Pally and Navi, my mother cooked a roast chicken dinner. As we all tucked into our meal laden with gravy, my grandfather, who was a vegetarian sat in stony silence eating his dal and roti.

On the morning of our move, my grandfather dragged Navi to the gurdwara with him even though he knew that she wanted to see us off. Piling our few sparse possessions into my dad's old Beetle, we left without saying goodbye to her. My grandfather's refusal to let Navi live with us would turn out to be one of the worst decisions that he'd ever make.

'My grandfather just wanted to suck the joy out of living for Pally and Navi. Sometimes they weren't even allowed to watch television. I remember Eurovision was on and it was the year that Bucks Fizz ended up winning. Usually we would sit down as a family and watch television shows together, like Laurel and Hardy or the wrestling on a Saturday with Big Daddy and Giant Haystack which was a must-see for all of us. But because my grandfather realised that Pally and Navi were desperate to watch Eurovision with the rest of us, he deliberately sent them to bed instead. Deliberately! On purpose! Just because he could!'

'You sound very angry Jas. I get the sense that your childhood was shrouded with anger.'

'It was . . . some of the time. Because there were enough unnecessary, stupid, soul-destroying, suck-the-joy-out-of-living-for-no-good-reason things happening that would have tested the patience of a saint! To stop his daughters from watching Eurovision! How fucking ridiculous!'

Fourteen

An Old Milk Crate

'You stayed up for thirty seconds! That was really good,' said Kamal.

I straightened up and grinned at my new neighbour. Kamal and I had been practicing handstands in the alleyway that ran along the back wall of the row of terrace houses.

Within a few days of our move, I realised that living in Walsall was going to be completely different to how we'd lived in Bentley. In Bentley, there had been no Indian neighbours and apart from our cousins, no other children in the neighbourhood to play with. But in our new street, every house apart from one was Sikh Punjabi and every house apart from one, was full to the brim with children of similar ages to me and my sisters.

Guneet, his wife Santo and their two children - a girl called Manny who was around my age and her younger brother - had moved next door to live with Guneet's brother Ram and his wife Lakhbir. While Guneet was always nice to me and my sisters, Santo who was arrogant and snobby, would look down her nose at us.

As I grew older, I came to recognise and avoid those women who disliked me and my sisters because we were a family of girls. The women in my large extended family fell into one of three categories: those like Santo who would openly denigrate me and my sisters, others who would make a feeble attempt to hide their disdain for us and then there were those rare examples like Ram's wife Lakhbir, who despite having only one child, a son called Narinder, was one of the nicest women that I'd ever meet. She always treated me and my sisters with kindness.

On the other side of our terrace house, with our kitchens facing onto each other's, there lived a strict and grumpy man called Dev, his wife Rani and their two daughters, Jaspreet and Randeep and their young son, Darshan.

Further along lived a very quiet woman with her husband (who I never saw), her two sons and two nieces who were two or three years older than I was. Grubby and unclean, the two nieces always looked as if they'd just finished crying. The other children in the street had quietly whispered from the corner of their mouths that we were not to play with those two girls or ask them about their mother. The rumour mill murmured a wretched tale that their mother had been taken to India and killed. Several months after we moved in, both girls disappeared.

The last house in the street belonged to Charlie, the only white man who lived in the short row of houses. Charlie's house was the only house that didn't have children. As soon as we moved in, my sisters and I were told by Darshan to stay away from Charlie because according to Darshan, apart from himself, Charlie didn't like children. Not particularly bothered about making friends with an older white man anyway, we stayed away. But one day I had wandered over to get my ball from Charlie's garden and he had come out of his house. Believing that he'd come to shout, I was surprised when he was chatty and full of smiles. But suddenly Darshan had raced across to us and had practically dragged Charlie back into his house, telling me to get out of Charlie's garden because I'd trampled over his vegetable patch whilst retrieving my ball. I knew I hadn't, but I didn't bother to argue with Darshan.

Although other children were allowed to wander in and out of our garden, my mother had forbidden me and my sisters from going into the gardens or houses of neighbours unless we were invited and we were never invited unless someone needed us girls to partake in an old Punjabi ritual called 'panj-kanjka.' The local Sikhs in the neighbourhood soon discovered that having five unmarried young girls in one household was very handy because it meant that they didn't have to go around all the houses knocking on doors to find the odd girl here and there to make up the numbers they needed – they just had to knock on my mother's door. It involved me and my four sisters attending at a house that had recently suffered an outbreak of measles, so that the household could pay homage to the goddess of measles by providing a meal for five unmarried girls. We'd have to sit on the floor, eat dal and roti, be presented with red chunnis and have our palms decorated with henna. In turn, the household would receive a blessing for this good deed from a local priest and the goddess of measles would be pleased.

Guneet had left a few pieces of furniture, beds and a settee, but we had very little kitchen equipment. Neighbours and relatives brought odds and ends that they could spare; plates, teacups and some cutlery. My parents borrowed some money from a relative and went to Walsall market to buy pots and pans and gradually our kitchen cupboards started to look less bare.

After sorting and settling in, my mother had allowed us outside to play and Kamal had ventured over to say hello. Kamal's house was next door to Ram and Lakhbir. She lived with her parents, three brothers and both her paternal grandparents. She was ecstatic when she'd discovered that five girls around the same ages as her had moved into the street. During the summer holidays, she'd appear at our back gate and wait patiently for us to come outside and play.

'Dinner's ready,' called my mother.

'See you tomorrow?' asked Kamal.

I nodded. 'Yeah, see you later.'

After dinner, Dimple and I washed the dishes, but we were both too short to reach the taps, so before we could start, one of us would go outside and fetch an old milk crate which was kept by the back door. Turning it upside down, we'd have to stand on it so we could reach the taps.

Dimple would scrub using Fairy and hot water, which she had to heat in a pan on the gas stove and I would rinse the dishes under the cold water. I had to use cold water because my parents only turned the hot water on once a week on Fridays for bath day. Once everyone had taken a bath, the hot water would be switched off again until the following Friday. Come summer or winter, in the mornings we had to wash our faces with freezing cold water.

We didn't have central heating and even in summer it would sometimes be too cold to sleep upstairs, so we would all sleep downstairs on the living room floor in makeshift beds, using the gas fire in the living room for warmth.

My sisters and I would pile the duvets and pillows at the top of the stairs, straddle the lumpy pile and push ourselves off. Sliding down the narrow stairwell, we'd inevitably smack into the wall at the bottom of the stairs. Ending up dizzy and tangled in the duvets, it was the only thing that made the chore of fetching down the makeshift beds enjoyable. In the mornings, we'd have to bundle up the duvets and pillows and take them all back upstairs.

The next morning, as Dimple and I stood on the milk crate and washed the breakfast dishes, feeling braver and confident Kamal ventured past our back gate and appeared at the back door.

'Wait a minute, I'm coming,' I called. Fingers already numb under the cold water, I rushed to rinse off the last few cereal bowls.

Kamal peered around the back door with a quizzical look. 'You're washing up?'

'We wash up all the time,' said Dimple, stepping down from the milk crate. 'Don't you wash up in your house?'

Looking amused, Kamal shook her head. 'Naw, my mum and grandma wash up.'

Dimple threw her a crocodile-smile. 'Don't worry, I'm sure that they'll make you do it soon. Then you'll realise how lucky you've been!'

I closed the cold water tap and stepped down from the milk crate. Dimple and I would get into trouble if we left the milk crate by the kitchen sink, so I picked it up and placed it back outside.

'I got this.' Kamal held up a cassette tape. 'Have you got a cassette player?'

Dimple nodded. Despite not having any cassette tapes, Dimple had assumed sole ownership of an old cassette player that Guneet had left behind.

'Will your mum shout at you if I play this at your house?' asked Kamal.

I frowned. I couldn't understand why Kamal thought that my mother would shout at us for wanting to play a cassette tape.

Dimple laughed. 'Don't you have a cassette player of your own?'

'Yeah, but my grandfather doesn't like it if I dance. He gets angry and shouts at me. I can teach you lot to dance if you like,' she added.

Dance? Both Dimple and I looked at each other.

We'd never danced before.

'You ask mum,' I said to Dimple. She was my parents' favourite and for some reason, it seemed that my mother went out of her way not to upset her. Dimple asked and my mother, looking bemused, said yes. With trepidation because we didn't know whether Guneet's old cassette player even worked, we plugged it into a socket in the living room and gingerly placed Kamal's tape into the hatch. Dimple pressed play and we all listened entranced as the sound of Alaap blasted out of the small speakers.

At the sound of bhangra music, Sarb, Pardeep and Bina rushed across to join us and within a few minutes Kamal was teaching us all how to dance. Starting with basic bhangra moves, we all soon cottoned on. Eventually we managed to persuade my dad to buy us our own Alaap tape from the Indian video and music store down the road and over the rest of the summer holidays, we gradually built up our collection to include Golden Star, Apna Sangeet and DCS.

Our house became the only one in the row of houses that played music. Any time the other girls in the neighbourhood wanted to dance or heard our music, they would hurry over. We didn't begrudge them joining us, because after Sarb and Manny had been dancing in our garden and Darshan's grumpy father Dev had thrown a steel pole at them, missing them by mere inches, we had realised then that Kamal's grandfather wasn't the only one - it seemed as if every other person wanted to drain the fun out of living.

'The joy of dancing has never left me. Anytime I feel down and depressed I get up and dance. By the time I was ten, Dimple and I were doing all of the chores in the house, washing up, cleaning and eventually doing the cooking as well. I can barely even remember a time when I wasn't doing chores, but none of that mattered because my parents allowed us to dance; we weren't banned like other girls. There are so many things I hate about the Indian

culture, but there are also so many things I love...bhangra and Bollywood makes all the rest of the nonsense just about bearable.'

'My parents were smart. They loosened enough of the leash around our necks so that we wouldn't feel aggrieved enough to have arguments with them or run off, but they still controlled us. In our new home, we had some new rules. We weren't allowed to look out of the windows or play with any of the neighbourhood boys and after school we'd have to change out of our uniforms straight away and come back downstairs. We weren't allowed to linger upstairs in our bedroom. My mother would call us down if she thought that we were taking too long getting changed. She constantly used the old doctrine of divide and conquer. Even though I was friends with my sisters, we didn't really confide in each other too much because my mother was a master at playing her daughters off against each other. When you have so many kids, you can be picky and swap your favourites around, depending on what you feel like on the day. My mother had assigned Dimple the role of surrogate mother and though the rest of us could tell each other our secrets, we never told Dimple because she was encouraged by our mother to tell on us.'

Fifteen

Same Stretch Of Road

'It's your first day at your new schools and all of you have promised not to cry, so as a special treat we'll have roast chicken and chips tonight,' said my mother as she fussed over my younger sisters.

The summer holidays were over. Sarb, Pardeep and Bina were starting at Alumwell Infant school while Dimple and I would attend the adjacent, Alumwell Junior school. In the distance along the same stretch of road stood a formidable building, Alumwell Comprehensive school which my aunts Pally and Navi attended. Named after 'Alum Well,' a once famous spring, the three schools weren't just connected by name, they also shared a vast green playing field.

My dad's work at the foundry had dried up, so my parents used clothing vouchers given to them by Walsall Council to buy new school uniforms for me and my sisters. All of our other everyday clothes and shoes were cast-offs from relatives and neighbours. Everything in our new home was basic and we made do with second-hand. The wallpaper didn't match the carpet, the settee didn't match the curtains and the few pictures on the walls were hung in no particular order or style. My parents didn't particularly care about décor - where every penny mattered, they only cared about necessity.

We were poor, but we never went hungry. Half of our back garden was used to grow vegetables and herbs and my parents would spend time planning our meals. Whatever my parents couldn't grow themselves, they would buy from Walsall market. We couldn't afford to buy groceries from the supermarket and we didn't need to, because Walsall market had fruit and vegetables that were always fresh and cheap. Biscuits were only bought for visitors or special occasions, but sometimes on the way back from the market, my parents would pop into Greggs and buy some jam doughnuts. They were five for £1, so it didn't take much for my parents to delight and treat me and my sisters.

I was eighteen before I realised that what the English refer to as a Sunday roast, was exactly the same meal that we ate on Fridays or Saturdays, minus the Yorkshire pudding. Roasted meat, roast potatoes, vegetables and heaps of gravy. For us, it was special because it was different from our usual meals of sabji, dal and roti. Being Sikhs, our religion forbid us from eating meat or drinking alcohol, but both my parents ate meat and they refused to let religious nonsense interfere with our diets. They only cared that my sisters and I were eating.

One of our relatives had given us an old television set and once we'd completed our homework, we were allowed to watch children's shows like Dangermouse, He-Man, Blue Peter, Take Hart with Morph and Grange Hill and once a week without fail we'd watch Dallas. The wealthy oil barons lived in a world very different to mine, but as a child I could never understand their constant fighting and never-ending conflicts with each other - if you had enough money to do whatever you wanted to do, then what was there left to fight about?

Now that my parents didn't have to do what my grandfather wanted, we celebrated Christmas, Easter and Diwali. My dad took Dimple with him to Walsall market to buy our very first Christmas tree. It was four feet high, artificial and had only eight baubles hanging on it, but to me it was the most beautiful Christmas tree in the whole world. On Christmas Day, we'd cook a big Christmas dinner with a turkey and all the trimmings and my sisters and I would get one Christmas present to share between the five of us. As the eldest, Dimple and I would always let one of our younger sisters unwrap the present. The present would usually be a board game such as Connect 4, Frustration or Buckaroo - my parents knew that we loved playing games and they always picked games that we could play together.

'My parents didn't even worry if we ate beef which is forbidden over and above other meats. The founder of Sikhism, Guru Nanak was born into a Hindu family and Hindus regard cows as a sacred animal, a belief that was transferred over from Hinduism to Sikhism. There are some gurdwaras in India and here in England that serve meat, but I could never eat meat under the same roof as the Guru Granth Sahib. Even thinking about it feels wrong, I can't really make any sense of why I dislike even the thought of it so much because I'm quite happy to eat meat everywhere and anywhere else!'

'Maybe it's been indoctrinated into you to think about a gurdwara in a certain way Jas?'

'I think you're right. Sometimes things being a certain way are fixed into our heads and we can't seem to shift or change that. I grew up with two very different versions of what it meant to be a Sikh. On the one hand we were Punjabis, who like to eat, drink and be merry. My dad, like so many of my other male relatives didn't wear a turban. But if we had any religious event going on in the gurdwara

or in our home, meat and alcohol would be banned and we'd become vegetarians for the entire period of the event. And then once it was over, we'd go back to eating meat and my dad would crack open his can of beer.'

'How did managing the two versions of Sikhism affect you Jas? Was there ever any confusion?'

'No, because I was raised with both versions. I experienced first-hand both sides. One side was easy-going, comical, fun, full of joy and music and the other was, well . . . although not entirely bland, it was a plain, limited and mundane existence. It seemed to be a life where almost every minute of every day, you were preparing yourself to go to heaven so you can't really live in the here and now if you're already consumed with your departure. Constant praising of God, only so you'd get into heaven, never really appreciating all that he'd created for you to enjoy while you were on this earth. Luckily neither of my parents wanted that kind of bland life full-time and they didn't make a big fuss during religious festivals or celebrations. We didn't have a lot of money anyway so everything had to be low-key. When we lived with my grandfather, me and my sisters had never been allowed to celebrate our birthdays. But once we moved to Walsall, on our birthdays my dad would buy a Victoria sponge cake from Walsall market and we'd all gather round to sing happy birthday. We never got presents though and we never asked for any, apart from on one occasion when I simply couldn't stop myself.'

Sixteen

£9.99 Please

'Dad, look at this picture! My friend from school got one of these for her birthday and today she let me hold it! Can I get one for my birthday?' I waved a page that I'd torn from an Argos catalogue under my dad's nose.

My dad glanced at the tatty piece of colourful paper. 'Here . . . let me see.'

Before someone or something else could divert his attention, I quickly shoved the wrinkled paper into his hands. 'It's a real life-size doll. She's just like a real baby, she goes to sleep and everything! Everyone's got one!'

My dad studied the page and he frowned. 'So this is what you've been pestering me about? A plastic doll?'

'But it's just like a real baby!'

'Jas, your birthday is months away and you know that we have no money.'

I fell silent. The fact that we were poor was a topic which was mentioned in our house at least once a week.

'I didn't get a moments rest until I went into town and filled out the forms for you to join the library. I thought I was going to get some peace after that because you'd have all the books you wanted, but now you're making a racket about this plastic doll!'

I chewed my bottom lip. My dad was right. When I'd finally held my new borrowing card from Walsall library, I didn't think that there was anything else left in the whole world that I wanted. But then I'd learnt about this new toy doll and for the first time in my life, I was smitten with something other than books.

But perhaps my embarrassed and guilty silence tugged at my dad because he handed back the tatty piece of paper to me with the golden words. 'I'll see.'

After the 'I'll see' from my dad, at least once a week I asked and begged in the same breath, but without fail I would be met with silence from both of my parents. I had never asked for any toy before and apart from on one previous occasion, neither me nor any of my sisters had ever received a new toy.

On that one previous occasion, my uncle Sandeep had collected Sarb from nursery school and on the way home he had bought her a windup musical toy television, the kind which plays a nursery rhyme and the picture goes round and round. Overjoyed and pleased as punch, Sarb was proudly showing it off to everyone, but my cousin Jaggy wanted to play with it and he just grabbed it. When she tried to get it back from him, he threw it out of an upstairs window and it shattered into pieces. Sarb had cried for hours and Jaggy had got whacked by a couple of the adults.

That being the only time any of us had ever received a new toy for ourselves, I wasn't expecting anything from my parents. But five months later, on the weekend of my tenth birthday, I was shaken awake by my mother.

'Jas, wake up! It's time to go and get your birthday present. After giving us no rest from it, now you're fast asleep! Your dad's going to take you into town. He has other errands to do there so you can help him with those too. Now quickly get ready and try not to wake up your sisters!'

I didn't need to be told twice. Quick as a lightning bolt I found myself dressed and riding with my dad in the Beetle. Down the hill, over the traffic lights and straight down a long road. Once we'd driven under the railway bridge, I knew we were in town.

'Stay close to me,' said my dad as we parked the car and began to walk along the main street. It was early Saturday morning, but lots of people were already milling around. We walked down the main street and then turned right and up into the marketplace. Market stalls of all different kinds were lined up along a steep cobbled hill and passing stall after stall, steadily we climbed higher and higher.

Eventually my dad stopped and stepped up to a toy stall. I stepped in beside him. Laid out in front of me were toys of every kind imaginable, but I was searching for the only thing that I wanted. As I scanned the stall, my eyes lit up - there she was, hanging on a rack with the other dolls along the back of the stall.

My dad told the stall owner that he wanted to buy a doll for me.

His blue eyes twinkling, the owner looked down at me. 'Ah . . . which one would you like, young miss?'

I stood on my tiptoes to get a better look at the dolls. I went through the motions of choosing carefully, knowing that I only had one chance to pick the right doll - and then I saw the one I wanted. I pointed. 'That one please.'

'This one?' The stall owner placed his hand on the wrong doll.

Quickly I shook my head. 'No, not that one, the one next to it. The one with the blue clothes.'

'This one?' Grinning the stall owner reached back and took the doll with the blue clothes down from the rack. 'Here you go miss!' He leaned over the counter and placed the doll straight into my hands before he turned to my dad. 'That'll be £9.99 please sir.'

I held my breath in case my dad changed his mind after hearing the price of the doll, but he didn't flinch as he handed over a crisp £10 note.

'Thank you,' I mumbled at the stall owner as he handed my dad his penny change. The stall owner gave me a quick wink and a wide grin as he turned to serve another customer.

Clutching my new doll, I slowly walked back down the steep hill with my dad. Amid the hustle and bustle of the market, we stopped to buy fruit and vegetables and a Victoria sponge cake from the cake stall before we headed back to the car.

Going to Walsall market with my dad was a completely different experience than going with my mother. My dad would buy only what he needed before we'd load up the car and head home, but my mother would stop and browse at almost every stall. My mother didn't drive and we didn't have enough money to take the bus so we'd have to walk back, our arms aching with the heavy weight of fruit and vegetables. Eventually to spare our arms and not caring if we looked odd, we resorted to loading our bags full of shopping into my sister Bina's old pram so that we could wheel our groceries back home.

I climbed into the front seat next to my dad and held my new doll in my lap. It hadn't come in a shiny, pink box like the dolls from Argos, but I didn't care. I was stunned, still in shock that I'd managed to get something that I had really, really wanted.

'My sisters still remember that doll and they all have the same question. How . . . and what did I do to persuade mum and dad to buy it for me?! And I always tell them that I don't know cos that was the one and only time that any of us ever got a birthday present.'

'And did you have to share the doll with your sisters?'

'My parents didn't make me share the doll, but since I wasn't being forced to hand it over and I was safe with the knowledge that I could always get it back as soon as I wanted it, I let my sisters play with it too. So even though it was my doll, it was still relatively shared. Growing up in my house, there was no time or space for any kind of self-indulgence, everything was hard-gained and then shared.'

Seventeen

A Small Price To Pay

'Jas, can I have that?'

I was about to push a blue straw into the silver foil cap of a small milk bottle. My hand hovering over the foil cap, I paused and glanced up. Mark was standing in front of me. He was one of the toughest boys in my junior class, but he had never spoken to me before.

Every morning during playtime, my teacher would hand out small milk bottles to some children, including me. I didn't pay too much attention to who did or didn't get free milk at playtime, but even I'd worked out that my teacher would usually hand out milk bottles to the brown children and one or two of the white children. I didn't like to drink milk, but my teacher would sometimes check to make sure that I hadn't wasted any.

I frowned. 'You want this?' I couldn't understand why Mark would voluntarily want to drink milk.

'Yeah. I'll give you this for it.' Mark opened his palm to reveal a shiny ten pence coin. He looked sincere and the coin appeared real.

'I can have that? For this?' I asked.

Mark nodded.

I looked around for our teacher. We'd both be in trouble if she saw us, but she'd already gone to the staffroom.

'Ok, here.' I handed the milk bottle and straw to Mark as he passed me the ten pence coin. Exchange completed, he promptly turned and bounded back across the classroom, weaving his way around the desks to join the other white children sitting at the far end of the room.

Bending down, I tucked the coin into one of my socks. I didn't have to drink milk and I'd been paid for not drinking it! I was delighted. I skipped out of the classroom and down the corridor to the tuck-shop. 'Can I have one packet of those crisps and two of 'em sweets please?' I asked the teacher on duty behind the counter.

Skipping back to my classroom with my goodies, I headed over to where Mark was standing surrounded by his friends. They were laughing and joking around. Mark held the half empty milk bottle in one of his hands.

'Here Mark,' I held out one of the sweets I'd just bought. A short curious silence descended on the group. Mark seemed surprised, but he reached out and took the sweet. I turned and skipped back to my desk.

I knew all of Mark's friends, but I didn't play or hang around with them because they were boys. Some of the white girls played with them, but these white girls seemed frivolous and silly, always playing up in class and horsing around, constantly trying to draw attention to themselves. One rainy playtime when we'd been confined indoors, one of the girls had sneaked into our teacher's desk, pulled out a large stapler and without any encouragement from anyone, she'd deliberately stapled her own finger before throwing her head back and laughing.

I had overheard enough of the white children's conversations to know that they played together outside of school. I wasn't allowed to play with any of my school friends outside of school. My life was segmented to such an extent that my home life and school life didn't overlap. I would walk through the school gates in the morning and that was my life and then I'd walk out of the school gates at the end of the afternoon and apart from homework, nothing about school came home with me. My school friends and teachers had nothing to do with my life once I was home and my parents never went to any of mine or my sisters' parents evenings or sports days.

A few days later, in the playground I was approached by Amelia. Amelia was a short, stocky white girl who wore big thick glasses. We were in the same junior class, but I tried to avoid her because I could never tell what kind of mood she'd be in. She was well-known for being pleasant one moment and then spiteful the next.

Amelia hissed into my face. 'Oi Jas . . . my cousin's going to beat up your sister!'

I stepped back. I couldn't imagine Dimple had done anything to get beaten up about, let alone anything involving Amelia's cousin. I frowned at Amelia. 'What? Why?'

'Cos I don't like her! You can beat up your sister if you like! Otherwise after school by the sandpit on Friday, I'll get my cousin to hit her!'

'I'm not hitting my sister!' I hurried away from Amelia, wondering whether I should tell Dimple that someone wanted to beat her up. Dimple may not even believe me and besides, Amelia could just be saying things to cause trouble. But as the week progressed, Amelia continued to come up to me, grinning as she told me again and again that if I didn't hit Dimple, then her cousin would. I didn't want my sister to get beaten up by Amelia's cousin who was the same age as Dimple, but I wasn't going to hit my sister just to please a horrid white girl.

After school on Friday, as I raced to the sandpit at the back of the playing field, I realised that Dimple was a few paces in front of me and I could see that Amelia was already waiting with three other girls at the sandpit. However her cousin, who was just as horrid as Amelia, was nowhere to be seen.

Out of breath I panted as I caught up with my sister. ‘Oi Dimple . . . don’t go down to the sandpit!’

Dimple shrugged me off. ‘Why not?’

‘Those white girls are going to make trouble, that’s why!’

‘Well let’s go and see what they do!’ Dimple brushed me aside and strode straight up to Amelia. ‘So where’s your cousin then? All day today she’s been saying to me that she’s got summat really important that she wants to tell me and that I have to come to the sandpit to meet her! So I’m here now...but where is she?!’

Taken aback by Dimple’s abrupt tone, Amelia glanced over her shoulder, but the girls that she’d gathered had already started to drift away. It took Amelia only a few moments to realise that her absent cousin had abandoned her and her friends were deserting her. Amelia was suddenly outnumbered and alone.

‘Well go on then! Tell me what your cousin was so desperate to tell me!’ demanded Dimple.

Amelia began to stammer. ‘I-I dunno . . . n-nothing.’

‘Nothing!’ Dimple scowled at Amelia. ‘Next time don’t waste my time, yeah?’ Dimple turned and marched back across the field towards the school gates.

I stayed where I was and watched as Amelia’s face turned a bright red and her eyes began to water. But as Dimple became a small dot in the distance, the girls who had drifted away started gathering again along with a new addition - Mark.

Amelia turned to him. ‘Hit her, Mark! She was saying things about you! Go on hit her!’

I knew Mark and Amelia played together and that he would take her side over mine. Even if I called Dimple for help, she was now too far away to hear me and I wondered if I should try and outrun Mark.

Mark looked over at me. His eyes quickly sized up what was happening and what could happen. He turned to Amelia and pulled a face as he shrugged. 'I'm not hitting no one, I'm going home.' And with that, he turned and jogged off.

I let out a sigh of relief, the show was over. But as I also turned to leave, Amelia hadn't quite finished.

'You paki!'

Feeling a sudden flash of outrage, I spun around, swinging out one of my arms. Whack! The back of my hand connected with Amelia's face. Her glasses flew through the air and landed on the grass to the sound of shocked gasps from her friends.

Stunned Amelia stepped back. Her face turning bright red, she threw her mouth wide open and began to wail. 'J-Jas hit me and . . . and she broke my glasses!'

I had never hit anyone at school before and I didn't know if I had really broken Amelia's glasses, but in a panic, I turned and hurried home.

My parents had already received a telephone call from my school by the time I reached home.

'Jas, your teacher said that you hit a white girl today? Is that true?' asked my dad.

I looked up at my dad, knowing that my words would hurt him. 'I-I did . . . but . . . only cos she called me a paki!'

A shadow shifted across my dad's face, but disappeared just as quickly as it had appeared. 'What does that matter? Do you know how many times I've been called names since I came to this country? If I hit everyone who'd ever called me a paki, I'd have been locked up God knows how many times! You have to learn to ignore the white people who are nasty to you. They want you to get upset and do things to them so they'll have an excuse to throw us out of this country and we don't want to give them any excuse! Do you understand?!'

I nodded silently at my dad. Unfortunately I did understand. My parents never let me and my sisters forget how lucky we were to have been born in England. So if we had to put up with being called a paki, then that was a small price to pay for being here. Though I didn't understand the why, from a young age I knew about the existence of racism. When we had lived in Bentley, to get to the local park we'd have to walk past a row of houses and there was one house in particular where, if the people who lived in that house were standing or sitting outside, they'd shower us with racist abuse. But relieved that it was only verbal abuse and not physical, we never retaliated, keeping our heads down, we'd quietly walk on.

I was aware that abuse and attacks could come at any time from anyone. Once I'd been riding Sonny's bike along the pavement in Bentley when a car had slowly driven up alongside me. Someone in the car had opened their window and thrown a half-eaten apple directly at me. The apple, thrown with such force had hit me on the side of my head, knocking me off the bike and making me scrape and bloody my knees and elbows as I fell onto the hard, concrete pavement. It may just have been someone who hated cyclists, but after that incident, I didn't go for a bike ride on my own again.

'I do think I've been quite lucky in that I've only been called a paki a few times in my life.'

'I find that very sad Jas, that you feel lucky to have only been called a paki a few times.'

I shrugged. 'To me that's just the reality of being a brown person in a white country. I remember this French girl joining my junior school while her mother was temporarily working over here and the teachers made such a fuss over her and she was given preferential treatment. I saw it so clearly how some people are more welcome because of the colour of their face and yet a brown person can be born here and still be treated like an unwanted foreigner.'

'But I don't think my parents and other Sikh Punjabi families that I knew tried to fit in or integrate with white people either. Some of the thinking behind holding themselves back was that by avoiding white people, you're not going to get racist abuse. I can understand that as a protective measure. Also people tend to surround themselves with people like themselves because it's comforting. People seek out the familiar, the comfortable, what they know, which is why they all gravitate together in one area.'

'My parents had physically left India. So mentally and emotionally, I think that made them, like so many other people that I know, even more determined to hang onto the old traditions and customs. They were afraid of being in a different country with a different culture and worried about what damage the English culture, which they looked down on anyway, could do to their Sikh Punjabi culture.'

'There isn't a single Sikh Punjabi family that I know who came to England for the love of the English culture. They all came for financial reasons. They didn't come here to openly and fully experience a different culture or change their mindset. They intentionally remain rooted in the mindset of the country they've left behind. My parents created an Indian way of living in the middle of England. I was born here and I've spent all of my life here, yet I was raised by parents who used the mentality of a Punjabi village in my upbringing. I do think me and my sisters got lucky that we had glimpses of western influence in our lives. I grew up watching Bollywood films - I've watched Disco Dancer about three hundred times - but my parents still let us watch stuff like Fame, Chips, Charlie's Angels and A-Team. My parents loved watching the A-Team, so they didn't completely live in a Sikh Punjabi/Indian vacuum. Unlike many of my aunts and uncles, who despite living in

England, tried to keep their children away from anything that was western.'

'How did this kind of upbringing affect you Jas?'

'I was split. At bedtime, we actually combined the Lord's prayer with one of our Sikh prayers using both languages, making one new long prayer. I was stuck between two cultures and I didn't fully belong in either one of them. I can't really describe it, I always felt like I was living in a country that didn't really belong to me. It wasn't mine, it felt borrowed. I knew that some white people didn't want us here, but I wasn't an Indian from India either. Yet I was raised as if my parents still lived in India. I was restricted in what I was allowed to say and think and I had no physical freedom. But I could clearly see the life that was out there. There was this constant quiet thought about this freedom that white people took for granted, but it was out of reach for me because my family were narrow-minded and more concerned about what the neighbours and relatives thought. In the minds of both my parents, daughters did not face the world head-on and explore it and have adventures. We were taught to firmly close the door to the outside world, told there was nothing good out there for us unless it was something to do with India.'

Eighteen

A British Drunk

'Girls, your masi is arriving from India in a few weeks. She's going to get married here so we've got lots of work to do before she arrives.' My mother puffed as she put her feet up onto the settee. Pregnant with her sixth child, my mother was out of breath.

Confused we all looked up from our homework. 'Who? A masi? What's a masi?' asked Pardeep.

My mother's face suddenly turned red. 'Goodness me! You don't know what a masi is! You all know the word for your dad's sisters, so how come you don't know the word for my sister!'

As my sisters and I continued to look confused, in despair my mother shook her head at us before she began to explain. 'Masi is the name for your mother's sister. I don't know why you girls don't know that already? Back home in India I have two brothers and two sisters. My middle sister is already married, but my youngest sister isn't married yet. She's coming here to get married. Now do all of you understand?'

We nodded and continued to listen silently as my mother gave us a long list of chores that we had to do to help her prepare for her younger sister's wedding.

Originally my mother had had high hopes that her younger sister could marry one of my dad's younger brothers, but it was not to be. The idea was promptly quashed by my dad's sisters, Pupinder and Bhav, who wouldn't even consider the marriage proposal put forward by my mother. My mother had been so upset and outraged that her sister had been rejected by my dad's family that she had immediately declared that 'come what may, she was going to get her sister married in England - even if in the process she had to throw her down a well!' I understood this to mean that my mother didn't care who the groom was or his situation, as long as he could get her sister a British passport.

My mother had searched high and low amongst all of our relatives, friends and neighbours for a groom for masi. Then she'd searched lower and then lower still - eventually coming up with a widower who had a glass eye, was slow in his speech and had been left on his own to raise three sons. His eldest son was only four years younger than masi.

The widower's family had taken both of my parents to one side and quietly cautioned them that he was an abusive drunk. But my mother only heard that he was a British drunk, who through marriage to her sister would secure her British citizenship and just in case the widower got snapped up by someone else, my mother promptly fixed the engagement.

As neighbours and relatives began to arrive to help with the wedding preparations, they all agreed how smart and helpful my mother was. A poor woman with five daughters of her own and with a sixth child on the way, she was still selflessly and tirelessly helping her younger sister marry and settle in England. And all without any help from my dad's family, who were already well settled here. How easy would it have been for them to have assisted my mother's poor sister, but they hadn't even lifted a finger to help, but ah never mind because my clever mother had managed to do it all by herself anyway.

'Do you think that masi has seen a photo of him? He just looks so ugly.' Turning away from the living room door, Dimple pulled a face and wandered into the kitchen.

The widower and his family had driven from where they lived in Wolverhampton to our house to finalise wedding details with my parents.

One of my aunts was standing at the stove making Indian tea and she scoffed loudly at Dimple's question. Using a rolling pin to crush whole cardamoms, clovers and some fennel seeds, she threw them into the pan of boiling water, along with several tablespoons of sugar before she turned to Dimple. 'Why would anyone show her a picture? She'll see for herself on her wedding day, it's not far now.'

I was still in junior school, but I already knew about the different types of marriages that took place in my culture. There was the love marriage where the parents would expect their daughter to be forever grateful and beholden to them for allowing her to marry a man of her own choosing. And if for some reason her love marriage didn't work out, it wouldn't even matter what the reason was for the marriage breaking down, she would have to prepare herself to never hear the end of it from her family. Then there was the arranged marriage where a middle person would introduce the boy's family and the girl's family and then both the boy and the girl would get an opportunity to say yes or no to the marriage proposal. And finally there were forced marriages where the girl (and sometimes the boy) would be given no choice and would be forced by various forms of coercion and threats, to marry whoever their parents had chosen for them.

A lot of girls, especially those from India, weren't given any choice who they married. Their parents and relatives would choose the groom, make the arrangements and the bride-to-be had no say or choice. Quietly marrying whoever her parents had decided that she'd marry. The desire to get British citizenship overrode any notions of love, romance or compatibility. Most marriages, especially those arranged from overseas, were organised without the bride and groom setting eyes on each other until their actual wedding day. Even then, until the wedding ceremony had been completed, the bride's face and sometimes the groom's face would be concealed.

I hadn't seen a photograph of my masi so I had no idea what she looked like, but she was due to arrive from India any day. And a few days after the visit from the widower and his family, my sisters and I returned home from school to find a petite and pretty young girl sitting on the living room floor surrounded by bright yellow, purple, green and orange Indian clothes that glittered as they sprawled and tumbled out of her open suitcase. She was not as beautiful as my mother, but nevertheless I could tell in an instant that this was not a match made in heaven.

After a sparse wedding, my masi moved into her new husband's house in Wolverhampton. My parents would insist that my sisters and I accompany them to visit her because seeing us girls cheered up my masi, but I hated those visits. The house always seemed sombre with long shadows falling into dusty corners. While their father was never present during any of our visits, his three sons would stand staring at us silently, sullenness etched on their faces.

Less than six months after masi's wedding, both of my parents rushed out of the house in the middle of the afternoon leaving me, my sisters and our new sister Ravi in the care of one of our neighbours. They were gone for the rest of the day and most of the night. When I came downstairs the next morning, I found my masi in the living room. She was lying on one of the settees with her head wrapped in bandages. She was surrounded by several relatives, all of whom immediately fell silent as soon as I walked in.

Trying not to appear shocked, I smiled. 'Hello masi.'

She managed a small, weak smile, but said nothing. As soon as I left the living room and went into the kitchen, I could hear the relatives murmuring again, but they were speaking in such low tones that it was impossible to make out what they were saying. Quietly I wondered what had happened to masi. Had something fallen on top of her head or had she tripped down the stairs and bumped her head? I couldn't ask my parents or any other adults about what had happened because my sisters and I weren't allowed to ask questions. If I wasn't told something, I had to assume that the adults didn't want me to know.

During the day there was a constant stream of relatives coming and going. It seemed that every other person had come to visit my masi, but I wondered why her husband hadn't come to see her. I could only hazard guesses . . . perhaps he had already seen her in hospital or maybe he was hurt himself or maybe he was busy getting the house nice and tidy for my masi's return when she was better. However by the evening as the visitors tailed off and our house became quiet again, he still hadn't shown up.

'Girls, you all have school tomorrow so go upstairs to bed,' said my dad.

I stood up to join my sisters, but my dad stopped me. 'Not you Jas. You're to stay downstairs. The rest of you are not to return downstairs for any reason. Do you understand?'

Obediently my sisters nodded and throwing bewildered glances towards me, they all disappeared upstairs. My mother closed the door firmly behind them.

'Jas, go and sit on the floor next to your masi,' said my mother.

Confused, I did as I was told. I had only just sat down on the floor next to the settee where masi was lying when suddenly there was a very loud knock at the front door. My dad immediately jumped to his feet and hurried through to the front room to answer the door. At last masi's husband has come to see her, but to my surprise, a policeman and a policewoman followed my dad back into the living room.

'Hello,' said the policeman, looking completely out of place in our small living room.

From my position on the floor, both police officers appeared larger than life. My mother and I both managed to mumble a greeting as my dad indicated to the police officers that they should sit down.

Taking a seat, the policeman turned to my dad. 'Did you manage to get an interpreter sir?'

Nervously my dad nodded towards me. 'I did, yes. We have my daughter here. She can speak very good English, better than most adults I know. You can ask her any questions in English and she'll ask her aunt in Punjabi and then she'll translate for you.'

Both police officers looked completely taken aback. Unsure they gazed down at me before they exchanged uncomfortable glances with each other. Their apprehensive faces were full of indecision as they exchanged what-should-we-do glances.

For a moment it seemed as though both officers were going to get back onto their feet and leave. Then the policeman cleared his throat and leaned down towards me. 'Are you alright to help us with this?'

I hadn't realised that this was why I'd been kept downstairs by my parents, but I nodded at the policeman.

The police interview lasted for over an hour. After the police officers left and I was excused by my parents, tired and shaken, I slipped into bed beside Sarb and

Pardeep. I tried not to disturb them, but they were both still wide awake.

'Why were the police here?' asked Sarb.

'What's happened?' asked Pardeep.

'It was nothing. Just go to sleep.' I didn't want to tell them. It was best that they didn't have the images that I now had imprinted in my mind.

In their dark and dreary house, shouting and yelling at her, masi's drunk husband had chased her up the stairs with a hockey stick. Catching up with my masi on the landing, he had slammed the hockey stick down on top of her head. She'd managed to scream out in punjabi, *'save me, save me'* - the only words she was able to say, before she collapsed and lost consciousness.

Two of her stepsons had rushed upstairs and they had managed to wrestle the hockey stick out of their father's hands, knocking him to the ground during the struggle. With an irate out-of-control father and blood pouring out of their stepmother's head, the boys had dialled 999. Sirens blaring, a police car had turned up for the drunk husband, while an ambulance had rushed masi to the nearest hospital.

A few days after the police interview, my masi beckoned me from the settee where she was lying.

Putting my doll down, I walked across to her. 'Do you need something?'

She shook her head and seemed to be overcome by some emotion, so I waited quietly for her to give me instructions. She cleared her throat. 'Thank you for what you did.' She pulled me into her arms and held me for a few moments.

As I quietly returned to play, I felt a warm glow inside, but I didn't understand why or what it was. It would take me several days to work out that my masi was the first person to hug me since my grandmother Mama had died.

'How did it feel not to have been hugged by anyone, not even your parents, for all those years Jas?'

'It felt like something was missing from the relationships I had, especially with my parents. I grew up surrounded by a huge family, but like a lot of parents, mine had the mindset that parenting was only a practical chore to feed and clothe their child so there was never any nurturing or emotional support. On top of which my parents would often tell me that I was useless. They only ever said it to me though, not to my sisters.'

'Maybe they told you that you were useless to keep you in your place and to stop you getting above your station. Though I get the sense that you were already quite a compliant child.'

'I was so used to obeying my parents that whatever they told me to do, I'd do it without question or argument and I never showed emotion or made a drama out of anything. I would just get on with it. I became used to my parents thrusting responsibility onto me. One summer, my mother called me in from the garden. She took me upstairs to the entrance of the attic and handed me a bundle of gold wrapped tightly in a red cloth (no matter how poor Indians are, somehow they always manage to accumulate gold). She told me to hide the red bundle somewhere in the attic, where no one else would be able to find it, but before she sent me up into the attic, she said that wherever I hide it, I'd need to remember and go and fetch it for her the next time she asked for it. My mother knew that I wouldn't breathe a word to anyone and I never did, not even to my sisters or my dad. I just got on with the job I'd been given before I went back outside to play in the garden again. Several months later, my mother asked me to retrieve the bundle of gold for her. I climbed down from the attic, handed her the gold and then went back outside to play. I never asked her the whys or whats.'

'So when does the child in you really get to come out and play Jas?' asked my therapist.

I shrugged. 'Once we left Bentley, I don't think I was ever really allowed to be much of a child again. Me and Dimple had a lot of responsibility for the housework and our younger sisters so I wasn't allowed to be giddy and frivolous. I wasn't raised to be carefree. My mother and every other Sikh Punjabi woman I knew had a saying that they'd use time and time again – 'the more you laugh, the more you'll cry.' So from a very young age, I wasn't allowed to laugh openly or express joy or delight in abundance. Every emotion, even laughter had to be controlled and contained. If we laughed and my mother thought that we were laughing too much, she'd stifle us with that saying - 'the more you laugh, the more you'll cry' – so we'd stop laughing, we'd shut up. My mother, whom me and my sisters all trusted because you know . . . she's our mother, she made us believe that we would get punished for laughing too much, that something bad was going to happen to us later . . . . that somehow the universe would even out the score by making us sad. There wasn't much chance to be fully a child anyway because so many serious things happened in my family. There wasn't time to be relaxed and untroubled. There's a side of me that's serious, discreet and very quiet. As a child, I was so quiet that I wouldn't speak unless I had something really important to say and my parents knew that about me. They knew that I held things together and that I wouldn't repeat what I'd seen or heard unless not speaking out would be morally wrong.'

Nineteen

What People Are Really Like

'Thank you sir, thank you very much. Yes, I'll see you on Monday at 11 o'clock. Thank you, bye. Bye.' My dad put the phone down.

My mother was standing and waiting at his elbow. 'Well? What did the solicitor say? Will he take the case?'

Looking pleased, my dad nodded. 'I'm seeing him on Monday. He said he's done lots of immigration cases before. I'll take masi with me to his office in town. We'll have a chat with him and see what he thinks we should do.'

'Do you want me to come with you?'

'What are you going to do there? It's a big problem that we have to sort out and you don't even know how to speak proper English. You'll only get confused and slow him down by trying to ask him pointless questions with your broken bits of English. You know what you're like when you start talking. You tell the longest stories and we've only got half an hour with him.'

Silently my mother turned away. As long as my dad was willing to put in the time and money to help her sister get British citizenship, she was prepared to ignore the slight from him.

After masi's statement to the police, her husband had gone to prison. She never saw him or any of her three stepsons again. However her application for permanent UK residence based on her marriage to a British citizen was still being considered when she had been attacked by her husband and she had started divorce proceedings against him in the middle of her application.

For the first time in their lives, my parents had to consult solicitors. Her sister being forced to return to India was my mother's worst nightmare. Masi's return would only serve to give my dad's sisters a chance to gloat about another of my mother's failings - her foremost failure of course, was producing so many daughters. So keen was my mother to retain dignity in front of my dad's sisters that she was determined to do whatever she had to do to prevent masi from having an embarrassing return to India.

Not only was my masi's future in the UK uncertain, but she was now devalued because she had been previously married and was no longer a virgin. Most Indian men were obsessed with only marrying virgins, so masi would be treated as second-class goods, only worthy of another divorcee or another widower or a much older man - anyone who agreed to marry her would be met with gratitude.

I had already seen the treatment dealt by the women in my family to one of my distant aunts. Her husband had run off with a white woman and she had subsequently divorced him. But on family occasions and gatherings, she was now placed at the back. In any discussions, her views and opinions would be swept aside by the other women. Clearly they felt that they knew better than she did because they still had hold of their husbands.

I had also heard the gut-wrenching tales of girls who had previously been married, but after the marriage had ended, even though the girl may have been completely faultless in it all, she would still be considered as spoiled goods because she wasn't a virgin anymore. It was hard enough for girls who had been born in England to remarry once divorced, but it would be even more difficult for someone in masi's position who had little to no education, was tangled in legal complications and didn't have British citizenship to booster her chances of securing a second husband.

Later that day, my mother sat with two of our neighbours as one of the neighbours recounted the sorry tale of the parents of one poor girl, who had, unknowingly and most unfortunately, chosen a gay man for their daughter to marry. Six months after the wedding, when the girl's parents had gone to visit her at her in-laws house where she lived with her husband, it was only then that the girl had managed to tell them. But even though she'd never had sex with her gay husband, the girl nonetheless once married, was now considered to be spoiled goods. Knowing that men who were bachelors preferred virgins and never-before-married girls, her parents had swiftly searched for a man who was also a divorcee for her second marriage.

'It's the girl's life that gets ruined,' said our other neighbour as she slowly shook her head. 'It's bad enough having an unwed daughter sitting at home, but then you have a daughter who is divorced and sitting at home!'

The first neighbour tutted. 'Who knows what people are really like?! They tell the world that they're one thing, but really they're another. It's only after parents get their daughters married off, that they realise what despicable people her in-laws and her husband really are. After the wedding is over, that's when you see the truth of her new family and her new husband, but by then it's too late. What can you do? Once the parents have done their duty and got their daughter married off, then married she must remain!'

My mother didn't even have the grace to look guilty. To disguise the fact that prior to masi's wedding, she had been warned by the widower's family that he was an abusive drunk, my mother gave a loud sigh. 'Remember that awful man from America?' she asked.

'Of course! How can anyone forget that?' The first neighbour's eyes lit up. She was barely able to contain her glee at reciting the tale of misfortune that had fallen on someone else's daughter. 'His parents lived over here and he was settled in America. He came to England pretending to be all nice and normal, like boys should be. And his parents were bragging to everyone about his big job and all the money he makes! Luckily for us none of our daughters were old enough for marriage and he ended up choosing a girl from up north. The girl's family spared no expense and went all out because they thought that their daughter was going to go off to America and live happily ever after. They incurred huge costs fulfilling the groom and his parents' wishes, giving them the big wedding that they wanted. Her parents gave them everything they asked for in the dowry and they asked for a lot!'

'Yes, it was a big dowry,' said my mother. 'Everyone was shocked because it was so extravagant, but most of the stuff like the brand new TV, new washing machine, sofas and dining room set were bought for his parents because they lived here so what was the groom going to do with all of those things!'

The first neighbour nodded. 'Of course it was all for his parents! He certainly wasn't going to cart everything all the way back to America after the wedding, was he? So his parents ended up with a house full of new things and he went back to America with his new wife. That poor girl had no idea who or what her parents had got her married to. The very first day, straight from the airport she walked into her new home and her new husband introduces her to his white girlfriend who was going to live with them!'

I sighed and closing my book, I left the living room. I already knew how this story ended. It had taken an entire month for the girl's parents to finally relent, giving in to her crying and begging on the telephone before they had eventually agreed to let her return home. But this girl wasn't a virgin anymore and her parents wasted no time in finding her another groom - a man from India who wanted to live in the UK. In order to get permanent residence, he was willing to overlook the fact that their daughter had been married before and wasn't a virgin.

My mother's match-making had ended with hospital stays, prison and with masi as a divorcee now. If masi attained British citizenship, her value would increase and my parents may be able to find her a groom, who for his own needs and reasons, wouldn't particularly care that she'd been married before.

'It doesn't really matter how many times a man has been married, but the minute a woman gets divorced or widowed, she's downgraded. Even more than what she was before, being a woman and already considered second-class to men and all that.'

'I'm sitting here listening to you Jas and it beggars belief!'

'Which part? The parents of these girls or the dickhead grooms?'

'Well, I'm just wondering what kind of pressure these grooms must have been under from their parents to do something like that?'

'People do all sorts of things to please their parents, but when you're about to fuck up someone else's life because you can't say no to your dear mummy and daddy, then that's a different kettle of fish. To me things like this are shocking, but not surprising. So what if a boy has to screw up some girl's life, if his dearest mummy is happy and she gets off his back about marriage, he really doesn't care about screwing over someone's daughter. They lie and

pretend to the girl and her family that he's happy to get married, but behind the scenes, the attitude is I'll get married to shut up my parents, but afterwards I'm going to continue to do what I want. Marriage is just like a contract that some boys will fulfill to please their parents and the poor girl has no idea, she's never told about his reluctance to marry her so she's clueless. His parents get a daughter-in-law to produce grandchildren for them, so the son has ticked that box and the pay-off for him is that his parents won't care who he's shagging outside his marriage. A lot of Sikh Punjabi men really do believe that they're more important and special than women.'

'From birth, most Sikh Punjabi women are treated differently to men, they aren't considered to have any worth to begin with and when you're not a virgin anymore, your status in the eyes of the community is lowered even further. So you need something that you can use as leverage to balance out that inequality and if my masi could get her British citizenship, then she'd have a golden card up her sleeve. She had exigent circumstances for her marriage ending so that was considered by the Home Office when they were looking at her application for citizenship.' I paused and sighed. 'There have been so many times when I've wished that I'd fucked up that police interview!'

Twenty

Saris And Bangles

'I need to talk to you two . . . it's really important,' said Dimple as she came rushing down the stairs. She hurried across to where Sarb and I were sitting on the living room floor playing Connect 4. Our game interrupted, we looked up at her.

'What's the matter?' I asked as Sarb and I both got to our feet.

Dimple had a strange look on her face and I knew immediately that something wasn't right.

Pulling us into a huddle, Dimple was about to speak when Pardeep walked into the living room.

'What're you guys whispering about?' She smiled, elbowing herself into our circle. 'Tell me, I wanna know too.'

Dimple hesitated, glancing from Pardeep's face, to Sarb's and then to mine. She swallowed hard before she whispered. 'I-I just saw dad and masi k- kissing upstairs in mum and dad's bedroom.'

I must not have heard her correctly. Frowning I shook my head. 'What?'

'I-I just saw them in mum and dad's room . . . dad and masi . . . they were kissing each other.'

As Dimple repeated the words, everything I knew and felt about my dad altered. I could hear a strange ringing in my ears as I felt a sudden rush of blood to my head. Feeling as though someone had punched me hard in my stomach, I was shocked. I saw the same look of disbelief, hurt and betrayal reflected in the faces of my three sisters. As our world came crashing down around our ears, stunned we all stood motionless for a few moments.

'Did they see you?' murmured Sarb.

Dimple shook her head. 'I saw 'em kissing and then I quickly ran downstairs to tell you lot.'

'You have to tell mum,' I muttered.

'What?' Dimple looked as though she was going to cry.

I bit down on my lip. 'We *have* to tell mum.'

But before we could say or do anything else, my mother blustered in from the kitchen, making us all jump. Worried that she may have overheard us, we quickly pulled apart, but making a beeline for her sewing machine, my mother hadn't noticed a thing.

'Dimple, Jas, one of you go and call your masi,' she said as she sat down at her sewing machine. 'Then all three of you need to start on tonight's dinner. I've taken the vegetables out of the fridge and put them onto the counter. Make sure you use those first before they go off.' Her back already bent over the machine, my mother moved two pieces of material underneath the sharp needle and into position ready to sew. With a slight pressure of her foot on the pedal, she'd transform the two separate parts into one.

Feeling sick to my stomach, Dimple and I nudged forward. Followed closely by Sarb and Pardeep, we stepped up to our mother's side.

Dimple's voice was barely a whisper. 'Mum?'

'What is it?' My mother's hand hovered near the on switch as she lifted her head and glanced up. Her eyes went back down to the material in her hand, but then just as quickly she bobbed her head back up again. She narrowed her eyes. The four of us had never gathered as one group at her sewing machine before.

'I-I just saw d-dad and masi k-kissing in your bedroom . . . both of them were kissing,' mumbled Dimple.

The four of us held our breaths and waited for our mother's reaction. She studied us for a brief moment. Her eyes passing over our faces. Then not uttering a single word she put her head back down, switched on the sewing machine and pushing her foot down hard onto the pedal as the loud whirl of the machine filled the living room, she began to sew.

'Mum . . . ?'

'All of you go and get on with your chores,' she said, not pausing her sewing.

We couldn't move.

Then my mother spoke again. Her head remained down, but her hands were trembling and this time I detected something in her voice. 'Don't tell anyone else what you've just told me about your dad and masi. Do you understand? Now all of you go and do your chores. Go on, I'm not going to tell you again!'

Confused my sisters and I hesitantly walked away from our mother. Maybe she didn't believe us or maybe she hadn't really understood what we'd just told her.

A few days later however, she caught them together herself. Walking into her bedroom cradling my sister Ravi who was asleep in her arms, my mother was stopped dead in her tracks by the sight of her husband and her sister in the bed.

Despite knowing that her husband and masi were having an affair under her roof, my mother didn't appear to be doing anything about it. Perhaps she had been conditioned to believe that she was powerless, raised to think that as a woman she was helpless. That men were to be treated, no matter how they behaved, as if they were Gods.

A few weeks later, my mother even left my dad and masi to run the house while she went to India to visit her middle sister. The trip was unplanned, but my mother's other sister was dying and leaving masi in charge of me and my sisters, my mother rushed to the airport.

With my mother gone, there were no barriers between masi and my dad. Worried I gathered Dimple, Sarb and Pardeep in the living room.

'We need to think of ways to keep dad and masi apart. I think one of us always needs to be in the same room as them, so they can't do anything.' As my sisters nodded in agreement, I proposed the idea of a Divorce Club. Even at that young age, we were all aware that women can be treated as disposable by their husbands and we didn't want our dad to divorce our mother and be with masi. But as we made matching badges and took an oath that we'd do everything in our power to keep our dad and masi apart, we had no idea that our dark and troubled world was about to become even more overcast.

'My mother could have gotten so many things from India - saris and bangles, pans and ornaments, but instead she imported a woman who would sleep with my dad. Being born into an old-fashioned, backward-thinking Sikh Punjabi family, me and my sisters would have suffered anyway, but we definitely suffered more because of the affair. So what do you do when the very people that are supposed to guide you through your life, teach you what is right and what is wrong . . . what do you do when these very people are doing wrong themselves?'

'What did you do Jas?'

'Well, I didn't blame my masi.'

'You didn't?'

Slowly I shook my head. 'While some of my sisters absolutely hated masi, they couldn't stand the sight of her, I felt sorry for her. I don't know why. I don't agree with blaming the 'other woman.' The blame, as far as I'm concerned, always lies 100% with the husband. He's the one who spoke the vows and made the commitment. If he doesn't give a shit about his wife and his kids, then why should some woman who he's shagging give a shit? She may not even know that he's married, the man always knows he's married though!'

'But in this case, your masi certainly knew that your dad was married.'

'Of course she knew and I'll admit that she's got no morals, but my dad bears 100% of the responsibility for cheating on my mother. Children have an amazing ability to forgive their parents for almost anything, but I never put my dad back up onto his pedestal after I found out about his affair. But I didn't hate him either. He was easy-going, quiet and calm.'

'Do you think your mother would have experienced your dad as easy-going and calm? I think she may have been experiencing a different side to your dad.'

'I'm sure she was. But here's the thing, because my mother was in pain, she began to deliberately inflict pain onto others and as her daughters, we bore the brunt of her hatred towards females. She'd snarl, bitch and snap at us and say the most unreasonable and ridiculous things. She would backstab everyone, becoming a toxic person who we all began to detest. But my dad never changed towards his children, he never treated us girls any differently. Of course it was easy for my dad, I get that. He was having his cake and eating it so of course he's gonna be ok and even though his affair became an open secret and all of my dad's brothers and sisters found out about it, even the neighbours knew, nobody really did anything. Not even my mother did anything to stop him.'

'I'm not trying to excuse your mother's behaviour towards you and your sisters because there is no excuse, but maybe she felt powerless to stop the affair?'

'My mother certainly wasn't powerless. She did nothing, not even to masi, the woman to whom my mother owed nothing. She could have done something because she had the support of everyone, my dad's brothers and sisters, the neighbours and obviously me and my sisters as well. But like a typical stupid Indian woman, who always needs a man around, my mother said the reason that she didn't throw masi out of the house was because she feared that my dad would follow her out of the door and then she'd be left to raise six daughters on her own and she wasn't prepared to do that because without a father to control us, me and my sisters would have turned into slags. That's the excuse she gave. To stop us from becoming slags, my mother felt that she needed to keep hold of my dad whatever price she had to pay.'

'How did it feel to hear that from your mother?'

'This is going to sound very weird, but I was so used to my mother blaming me and my sisters for all the things in her life that were wrong, that on the one hand it was like water-off-a-duck's-back, but on the other hand, I felt angry. My mother was using me and my sisters as an excuse. She had her own plan which isn't how we'd usually see an affair being dealt with by the scorned wife. Her plan was that if my dad was going to sleep with her sister, then the least they could do was provide her with something. Her compensation for my dad's affair with her sister was that they were going to gift her a son!'

Twenty-One

My Mother's Place

'Girls! Can all of you come here, right now!' One evening, my mother called me and my sisters from around the house.

Several months after Dimple had first caught my dad and masi kissing, my mother who was back from India after her sister's funeral, asked us all to gather in the living room. Leaving my homework, along with my sisters, I sat down on the living room floor. All of us were puzzled and wondering why we'd been summoned together. Nothing like this had ever happened before. While masi was nowhere to be seen, my dad and my mother were sitting next to each other on the settee.

My dad waited until my sisters and I had all settled ourselves down before he spoke. 'Your mum and I are going to get a divorce.'

In the stunned silence that followed, he cleared his throat several times before he spoke again. 'After that, I'm going to marry your masi.' He glanced across at my mother. 'It was your mum's idea so we can finally have the son we've always wanted.'

I couldn't believe my ears. When my mother had rushed to India because her middle sister was dying, while she had been away, masi had taken the opportunity to pull out all of my mother's best Indian clothes, dress herself up and take photographs in different poses. Not content to simply pretend that she was the lady of the house, now masi was literally going to take my mother's place.

I had been hoping to be told by my parents that masi was leaving our house, especially since my sisters and I had managed to catch her and my dad together several times. On one such instance, we'd returned home from school to find ourselves locked out of the house. My dad and masi had bolted all of the doors and windows from inside to make sure that they weren't disturbed. We'd had no choice, but to wait outside until they came downstairs. When they unlocked the back door to let us in, they both acted as if nothing untoward was happening.

Now at the news of my parent's divorce, I gritted my teeth. My mother thought of the most stupid things! Coming up with the idea that her sister should marry her husband just to bear a son for her - my desperate mother! As if that child - and my dad and masi may never have a son together - was ever truly going to be my mother's child. As if masi, the sort of woman who only ever took, never gave, would if or when the time ever came, just quietly hand her child over to my mother.

The affair was a betrayal and a shot in the heart, but the idea that my dad would marry masi so that they could produce a son to give to my mother was ludicrous. My sisters and I sat in shocked silence watching my mother's face for any sign that a cruel trick was being played on us. But even though my mother was smiling, this wasn't a joke. My mother was grinning as if she'd found the most perfect solution to all her problems.

She nodded. 'This is the best way for me to have a son. Your dad and masi will get married and then they'll have a son. Once they've had a boy, then they'll get divorced and your dad and I will get married again.'

'Divorce masi?' Shaking his head, my dad frowned at my mother. 'That's not what we'd decided. Once I marry masi, I won't be divorcing her. I thought you understood that...and had agreed. I'll divorce you, marry masi and then that's the way it would remain. I'm not going to divorce masi and remarry you.'

The smile on my mother's face instantly vanished and something flashed in her eyes as she flushed a deep red. 'If you're not going to divorce masi afterwards, then I'm not going to agree to this plan!'

My dad cleared his throat as if he were about to speak. He opened his mouth, closed it, opened it once more and then closed it again without saying a word.

As my sisters and I began to shuffle on the floor, my mother turned to us. 'Well . . . that's all your dad and I wanted to tell you girls, but nothing is going to happen now. We're not getting a divorce. You can all get on with your chores or go and finish your homework.'

'If anyone ever wants to know the worst and most disastrous way of doing something, then just ask my mother! She'll tell you in an instant how to fuck up! The older I got, the more I realised that my mother was unhinged and unfortunately she was in a position where decisions she made affected others.'

'But in a male dominated culture Jas, why did your dad let your mother scupper up his plans to marry masi?'

'Because if my dad had divorced my mother and married masi and then remained married to masi and of course the third part of that stupid plan did not have my mother's blessing or support, then my dad's family would have disowned him. I didn't know it at the time, but my dad's family were working away in the background trying to sort out this mess. They wanted masi to be thrown out of

our house immediately, but of course in the middle of this big mess, there was my mother's motive and her desire for a son and the mess became complicated. My dad stayed, not because he loved my mother or any of his children to the ends of the earth, but because he would have been disowned and disgraced by his brothers who had told him straight that he couldn't ever leave my mother. But just because he couldn't leave my mother, it didn't mean that my dad was going to let go of masi either.'

Twenty-Two

Hoping For Something Different

'Girls? Didn't you hear what I just said to you?' My mother looked down at us. My sisters and I hadn't moved from the living room floor. 'Go and do your homework or your chores. I've already told you that nothing is going to happen. We aren't going to get divorced now!'

As my mother dismissed us with a nod of her head, somewhat reluctantly I stood up and my eyes locked with those of my sisters as they too slowly got to their feet.

I had been hoping for something different from my parents - that they would have been able to solve the problem of masi. If my parents weren't going to get divorced, then the next logical step would have been for masi to be removed from our home, but it was clear that nothing like that was going to happen.

Defeat and dismay clouded mine and my sisters' faces. I exchanged no words with my sisters as we drifted back in a daze to our homework and chores. Without needing to say any words, we all knew that the intentions and motives of the adults in our lives could disrupt and shake our family to its very core. My sisters and I would never be able to overcome or solve these problems, no matter how many badges we made or oaths we took.

Quietly and without any fuss or ceremony, we closed down the Divorce Club and threw away our badges. But the problem of masi and my dad could not be cast aside so easily.

Masi continued to live with us and my mother carried on treating her as if nothing untoward had ever happened or was happening. Me and my sisters were left with no choice, but to follow our mother's lead and we had to carry on interacting with masi as if nothing had ever been seen, said or heard. A part of me believed that because my mother was treating masi like normal, perhaps the affair was over, but I was mistaken.

It would take three years for my masi to secure British citizenship. On the strength of the police statement and my parent's efforts with the immigration solicitors, against the odds she managed to attain British citizenship. As soon as she did, my parents were able to find her a groom who hadn't been married before.

Masi's second husband, whom my sisters and I called masar, was from India. Around the same age as masi and not a big drinker, he seemed to be a better match for her than the widower.

Shortly after their wedding however, masi's second husband would claim that he hadn't been told before he had married masi that she'd been married before and was a divorcee.

Both my parents had scoffed at his claim. 'What nonsense! Of course we told him that masi had been married before. Well, we didn't actually tell the groom or his family ourselves, but we told the middleperson. It's not our fault if the middleperson didn't pass that information onto the groom and the groom's family! And anyway so what if he wasn't told? Even if he had known that she'd been married before, it's not as if he would have turned her down! He needed a British passport, didn't he? He'd have married her regardless and now he's talking as if he's been hard-done by! After he married masi, he got his permanent stay in the UK and he was able to bring his parents from their tiny village in India to live over here too. He's forgetting all of that!'

Masi moved to Leicester with her new husband, but my mother was still so concerned about keeping up appearances that she would make Dimple, Sarb and I take turns spending our summer holidays in Leicester looking after masi's first baby, a girl.

'Everything was buried and we all had to carry on as if nothing had ever happened or been said. And sometimes that's the only way because what's already been done, can't be undone. Especially when there can be no resolution because the adults were going to do whatever they wanted to do regardless. Both my parents behaved as if nothing had ever happened. As children, there was nothing else we could do and like I've said before, there were so many other serious things happening in my family, that there really was no time to dwell on just one terrible thing.'

'But oddly, never once was there any drama or screaming matches or yelling or hair-pulling, despite the fact that one woman is sleeping with another woman's husband under her own roof. When I look back now, there was so much self-control, even from me and my sisters because none of us ever played up or showed to masi's face that we disliked her. I'd been raised to never show my feelings or emotions because they weren't considered important and it just reinforced the whole notion of putting-on-a-fake-happy-face and getting on with things. My mother never showed her disapproval or upset openly at masi, so how could me and my sisters? We weren't in a position to shout and scream at masi when my mother didn't. And because my mother carried on behaving

outwardly normal towards masi, it kinda showed me what a wife does if her husband is having an affair - she just stays quiet and does nothing. In other words, she puts up and shuts up. Once my sisters and I closed down the Divorce Club, we never sat and had any further discussions about the affair either. We just buried it even though it was still going on. We all went very quiet and silently carried our own pain. My sisters and I have many flaws as individuals, but none of us would ever dream of cheating or having an affair. I think that's as a direct result of my dad having an affair and the pain we all felt - I remember the pain like it happened yesterday. I was too young to understand about sex and although my sisters and I knew and saw some things together and saw some things separately in bits and pieces, only my mother knew the whole truth and it would take decades for the entire sordid tale to fully unravel.'

'Once again Jas you're dragged into problems created by the adults around you. That conversation that your parents had with you and your sisters about your dad divorcing your mum and marrying her sister so they could have a son. How did that make you feel?'

'The pain was unbearable and it was raw because both of my parents were in the wrong. Their moral compass was pointing in the wrong direction and the blame for the affair somehow ended up being laid sideways at the feet of me and my sisters. It was framed by both of my parents as being about my mother wanting a boy and rightly or wrongly, I felt partly responsible and guilty for what was going on. I was made to feel that gaping lack of a son so deeply by my parents that once I even made up a story at school about having a brother, such was my desperation to fill that void. But the seed of that void was planted and took root because of my parent's constant complaining and statements about not having a son. By my mother's own account, if only I had been a boy, then she wouldn't have gone on to have six daughters. She'd have stopped at two children and then of course she wouldn't even have had to

think about getting my dad married to her sister in order to get a son.'

Twenty-Three

Like A Boy

'Bina! What's happened to your hair?'

At the sound of my mother's shriek, I looked up as Bina wandered into the living room. Her long dark hair had been chopped right up to her ears.

Unassuming and passive, my sister Bina barely ever spoke above a whisper. Smiling she shrugged. 'The neighbour cut it,' she murmured. 'She said because you had another girl, if she cut my hair, then I'd look like a boy.'

For once even my mother was speechless.

After my sister Ravi was born, my sisters and I had endured weeks of endless visits from relatives, friends and neighbours. Holding the new baby, they'd slowly shake their heads from side to side and tut from the corner of their mouths, sometimes throwing accusing glances across at us as if somehow my sisters and I were responsible for the birth of my mother's sixth daughter.

'See! Another witch has been born into this house!'

'Now he's got six daughters. It's too heavy a burden for any man to bear, but especially for one who's poor!'

'How can one man marry off his six daughters?'

'A couple of them should've been drowned at birth!'

We listened quietly as we served tea and biscuits to our well-wishers.

Not wanting to argue with the neighbour, my mother tried to make light of Bina's haircut, knowing that what had been done couldn't be undone. But the Punjabi school teacher at the gurdwara had plenty to say to my parents about Bina's haircut, calling to lecture them on the virtues of Sikhs keeping long hair.

Bina and my cousin Banita attended Punjabi classes on Sunday mornings at Pleck gurdwara. When we'd lived in Bentley, my sisters and I, along with Pally, Navi, Sonny and his brothers had attended Punjabi classes at Willenhall gurdwara. But we had all complained so much and so loudly every Sunday morning, that for once our parents had eventually admitted defeat. Only Bina and Banita had wanted to continue learning to read and write Punjabi.

Three weeks after Bina's haircut, she came home in tears from the Punjabi school. 'The girls keep saying things about my hair and asking why I got it cut and I don't know what to say to them,' she sobbed. 'I thought they would stop after the first week, but now they're saying horrible things about mum and dad. They said we ain't proper Sikhs cos mum and dad cut my hair. The teacher didn't even say anything to them, he was laughing at me too!'

Children of mixed ages were taught in the same classroom at the Punjabi school because there weren't enough students for classes to be split according to age and ability. Bina, being one of the youngest and the quietest was an easy target for some of the older girls.

'Shall I join the Punjabi school?' I asked my mother. 'I could speak to the girls and tell them to leave Bina alone.'

My mother narrowed her eyes at me. 'Are you going to sort it out?'

I nodded. 'But I'm only staying until it's sorted.'

'I wanna go too,' said Sarb.

My mother agreed and the following Sunday, with no real clue of how I could 'sort it out' I joined the Punjabi class with Sarb and my cousin Japdeep who happened to be staying with us for the weekend. We didn't tell anyone in the class that Bina was our sister. We sat silently, watching the teacher laugh along as a group of six older girls, around the same age as I was, teased Bina.

When the two-hour class was over, Bina, Banita, Sarb, Japdeep and I headed downstairs to the girls' cloakroom. We'd just finished putting our shoes on when the group of girls who'd been teasing Bina walked into the cloakroom. Spotting her, they immediately made a beeline for her, trying to surround her.

I quickly stepped in front of the girls, stopping them in their tracks. 'Excuse me . . . you need to leave my sister alone.'

'Your sister? What're you on about? Who's your sister?' The girl at the front of the group gave me a confused glare.

I nodded towards Bina. 'That's my sister.'

'Your sister?'

I nodded again. 'Yeah and her hair has got nothing to do with you lot, so you need to stop going on about it!'

'Why's her hair so short though?'

'What's it got to do with you? She's not saying or doing anything to you lot so you just need to leave her alone, yeah?'

'Who's gonna make me? You?!' The girl laughed as she inched forward.

I realised we were outnumbered as the rest of the girls in the group stepped up behind her. 'Just leave my sister alone. That's all I'm saying,' I said.

But nudged forward by the girls behind her, the girl stepped up to me.

I took a step back. 'Don't come any closer, yeah?'

But the girl leaned forward, pushing her face into mine and though it hadn't been part of any plan, instinctively I punched her on her nose.

Eyes shocked and full of unexpected pain, she reeled away from me, holding her hands to her face as blood started to pour out of her nose. The girls' cloakroom instantly emptied as she and the rest of the girls in her group turned and scrambled, one after the other out of the door, pushing and shoving each other aside in their haste to escape and get away.

Watching them all disappear out of the cloakroom, I didn't know where they'd gone or what they would do next, but I wasn't going to hang around to find out. I turned to Sarb, Japdeep, Bina and Banita. 'Come on, let's go! We have to get out of here!'

We headed straight out of the main doors of the gurdwara and running as fast as we could, we were already halfway home when we realised that we were being chased by a mob of teenage boys.

'Oi! Wait up!'

'You hit my sister!'

'Wait til I get you!'

I could hear the boys shouting, but I didn't stop. 'Come on! Run faster!' I panted to Sarb, Bina and Banita. Japdeep had been raised with three brothers, so I knew that she was more than capable of holding her own, but both Bina and Banita were too small to fend off a gang of teenage boys.

'Oi! Wait 'til we get hold of you! Ya bitches!' The boys continued yelling as they began to gain on us.

We were almost home so I broke into a faster run. I threw myself at our front door. Bang! Bang! Bang! I pounded my fist on the wood as hard as I could. My mother swung the door wide open just as the boys came around the final corner.

'Mum . . . mum . . . those boys are coming to get us!' I managed to pant.

My mother stuck her head out of the front door and spying the boys, she quickly stepped out onto the pavement. Taking off one of her house slippers, she raised it high above her head and then shrieking at the top of her voice, she rushed past my sisters and cousins and headed straight for the teenage boys. 'Come on then! Let's be having you! I'll sort you out! Wait there! Come on over here! Let me sort you out!'

As the boys realised that they were now dealing with an irate adult, they skid to an abrupt stop and began tripping and stumbling over themselves as they attempted to quickly retreat and turn back. Shouting and waving her slipper above her head, my mother chased them all the way back down the street and around the corner.

With aching sides, we collapsed into laughter when after a few minutes, my mother came back around the corner. Even though the boys had long disappeared, my mother was still shouting.

Out of breath she laughed as she came inside. 'They should have waited! I'd have sorted them out good and proper if I'd got my hands on them! Chasing my daughters indeed!'

'It was hilarious at the time and it's still funny even now whenever I think about it. That was one of only a handful of times that my mother had stuck up for her daughters. The rest of the time, my mother didn't really care too much about us, we weren't raised up so much as dragged up.'

Twenty-Four

A Good Thing

'Follow me girls. Quietly now,' said Miss Bates.

Having separated the girls from the boys, my teacher Miss Bates escorted all the girls in my junior class to a mobile classroom at the far end of the playground. Leading us into the room, she indicated that we should take our seats before she promptly departed. As I sat down, I noticed at the front of the classroom that there were two women who I had never seen before, standing and waiting patiently for us to settle down.

'Ok girls, quieten down please. Right then. Let's begin, shall we? Hello girls. We're here today to talk to you about menstruation. Now do any of you know what menstruation is?'

Two white girls immediately shot up their hands. I'd never heard of menstruation, but as the two women began to hand out small booklets and I listened to them explaining about periods, tampons and pads, I felt nothing but sheer disappointment.

Up until now, I'd always believed that before children were fully grown, they had the ability to choose between becoming an adult or changing into an animal. I loved Black Beauty and instead of becoming an adult, I felt that I'd much rather spend my life running free and untamed. So I'd already decided that when the time came, I'd become a horse.

As I continued listening to the two women, waves of despair washed over me. What I'd always believed was within my grasp, was in fact impossible. I didn't have any choice about becoming an adult after all. My glum feelings were magnified by the realisation that there was nothing special or magical whatsoever about humans.

Later that day, after I returned home from school, I showed the small booklet to my mother. 'My school gave this to all of the girls to read.'

My mother gave the leaflet a brief glance. 'You're not to read this. Go and throw it in the bin.'

I felt a sudden flash of anger towards my mother. I had every right to know things about my body, but I didn't argue or say a word to her. Instead I walked into the kitchen and making out as though I'd thrown the booklet away, instead I quickly sneaked it back into my school bag.

That evening, after I'd done all of my chores, I took out a large reading book. I opened it to somewhere in the middle and placing the small booklet inside, I managed to read it from cover to cover right under my mother's nose.

A couple of years later, I noticed that after every visit from my masi and her husband - who worked in a factory in Leicester that produced toiletries, sanitary and hygienic products - a large plastic bag that had silently appeared in the bedroom wardrobe was quietly refilled with quality control failed and rejected sanitary pads.

'I get the sense that you've remained untamed Jas, despite everything that's happened to you.'

'I think the core of me has remained untamed. After I found out that I wasn't going to be able to change into a horse, I was kinda ok with the thought of being a woman. When my mother was young, in India they didn't teach girls about menstruation and certainly not about sex. I'm not sure about the education in the cities, but I do know that they didn't teach it in the villages. Periods were treated as a punishment from God for something or other, so they're not discussed or explained with openness. They're hidden away and treated like some kind of terrible illness or a curse. Its men who gave periods that stigma, but it's women who continue following that stupid way of thinking. What should be considered as a good thing because it's just another function that the body performs and a very important one at that, instead it's made out to be some sort of punishment. Sometimes I think that everything to do with women is turned into a negative by uneducated moronic idiots who prefer to live in the dark ages.'

Twenty-Five

Never Forgotten

'Are you seeing this Jas? Look at what they're saying!'

'Did you hear that? It's so terrible!'

I was playing with an old Sindy doll on the living room floor, but I lifted my head to see both my parents gesturing towards the television. Watching the BBC news at 9pm had become part of my parents evening ritual.

My dad's eyes were transfixed on the screen as he slowly shook his head. 'Look how awful it is.'

I set my doll aside as I sat up to focus on the flashing images beaming out from the television. On a street somewhere in London, a reporter with a big microphone in his hand was standing facing the camera with a solemn look on his face.

I felt a sense of sadness and disbelief as my ears took hold of his words. A policewoman had been shot and killed outside the Iranian embassy. A photograph of a young, smiling white woman in a police uniform flashed up onto the screen.

Once I'd realised that I wasn't going to be able to magically transform into a horse, I'd decided that I would become a policewoman instead. But as the BBC reporter talked on, I sat muted. I'd had no idea that policemen and policewomen could actually die. I'd always believed that they were invincible.

'Are you watching Jas? Look at what's just happened to that poor girl! Someone shot her. See how dangerous it is to be a policewoman,' said my mother.

'It's not safe. You're not going to be a policewoman,' said my dad.

I pulled my eyes away from the television and towards my parents.

My mother shook her head and tutted. 'You see, it's not a good job. We thought that it would be, but it's too dangerous. You can't be a policewoman. We don't want you getting killed.'

I picked up my Sindy doll again and pretend walked her along the carpet as I mulled over what I'd just learnt. At the age of ten, I trusted my parents and feeling jolted by the photograph of the young smiling policewoman who was now dead, I glanced across at my parents.

'Ok,' I said, but as I returned to playing with my doll, my parents had grasped the fact that without question or resistance, I'd listened to them about my future.

'I've never forgotten Yvonne Fletcher. It's strange that an event which didn't even have anything to do with me changed my course in life and I decided to become a journalist instead.'

'Your parents didn't have any objections to you becoming a journalist because that can also be a dangerous occupation, can't it?'

'They didn't say anything actually. My parents allowed me to have some dreams because it was easier than telling me upfront what they were really thinking about my future. At the time, it never crossed my mind that when I gave up one thing because my parents told me to, it was throwing

the door wide open for them to order me to give up other things.'

Twenty-Six

Six Dowries For Six Daughters

'We gave up that house and we left with nothing! My father-in-law threatened to throw us out so many times, so what choice did we have but to eventually leave,' said my mother.

Sitting next to one of our neighbours on the settee, my mother sighed. 'No one asks for daughters, but I've ended up with six to spare! I feel sorry for their father, he has to carry such a heavy burden. I constantly pray for one son . . . just one. It's not a big thing for God to grant me my wish, is it?'

My mother liked getting sympathy and the neighbour obliged. Shaking her head and giving a compassionate tut out of the corner of her mouth. 'Yes sister, you're right. Just one son would cover all of your six daughters. No one would even notice them then.'

'I know, one son would cover all of my girls, but it seems as if God is intent on punishing me for my past sins!'

I didn't even wince as I placed two cups of piping hot tea in front of my mother and the neighbour, who had two sons and no daughters.

Having delivered the tea, I retreated back to the kitchen. I had grown accustomed to leaving the living room whenever anyone came to visit because inevitably the talk would turn to how awful it was that my parents had six daughters. Having heard the same thing many times over, I preferred to leave my mother and her visitors to themselves as they begrudged mine and my sisters' existence. But in our small terrace house, conversations could still filter through into other rooms especially if those speaking weren't particularly bothered about who overheard.

'What're you going to do when they all get married?' I heard the neighbour ask. 'You'll need six dowries for six daughters! What a thing to have to think about!'

'Well!' said my mother. 'We'll have to say no to any proposal that comes along if the boy's family want a dowry. But surely before they open their mouths and ask us for anything, they'll know, won't they? They'll know that after raising six daughters, we won't have any money left for dowries or big weddings!'

'Have you thought about marriage proposals from India? Some boys from there are so desperate to come here that they won't even ask you for a dowry. You'll get no end of proposals!'

'Oh no! Absolutely not!'

Grateful for small mercies, I smiled softly. My parents had always been adamant that neither I nor any of my sisters would marry anyone from India.

'But what's wrong with boys from India?' asked the neighbour.

'Oh you know what they're like! The boy will do whatever he needs to do to get a British passport and then once he's got that, then he'll do whatever he wants to do! He'll send all of his money back home to his family in India or he'll bring all of his family over here and he'll spend his whole life running around after them and looking after their demands!'

'Don't you think that you're making your lives difficult for no reason? Boys from India are not all bad.'

'The way you're talking, I'm beginning to think that maybe you've got a boy from India up your sleeve for one of my daughters!'

The neighbour started to chuckle. 'Now that you mention-'

'Drink your tea before it gets cold,' said my mother.

There was a short pause before I heard the neighbour again. 'Ah, this is lovely tea. You've taught your daughters well.'

'Of course! I don't want any of my daughters' future in-laws sending me complaints after they're married, do I? I tell my daughters all the time about not being useless. If they are and I tell them off, it's only for their own benefit that I'm saying these things. I'm teaching them all the skills that they'll need to become good wives. A girl needs to know everything to do with the kitchen, how to prepare and cook meals, how to clean the house and how to sew and mend. I take my eldest daughters with me to sewing class every Saturday at that school down the road. They need to learn how to mend and make clothes.'

Silently I rolled my eyes. What my mother had neglected to mention to the neighbour was that just like the Punjabi classes that we had refused to attend, the sewing classes were even more disorganised and taught by a woman who would use them as a chance to spread gossip. I hated being dragged along to the sewing classes by my mother. I was a girl and on that basis alone, according to every woman I knew, of course I should know how to sew. There were no boys in the class. If any of the other women had to bring their sons along with their daughters, the boys were allowed to play football outside while the girls were stuck indoors listening to gossip and the mindless chit-chat of the women as they haphazardly waved scissors around.

My mother continued. 'But most importantly, my daughters will need to know how to time-pass because whatever else happens, they'll have to do that.'

The neighbour sighed. 'Ah yes, time-pass. That's what your girls will have to do. That's what we all do, isn't it?'

My smile vanished as I clenched my teeth. I seethed with frustration at hearing women talk about time-passing!

Time-pass meant passing time - a phrase used by most of the women that I knew. I translated it as - 'keep your mouth shut and quietly and dutifully for the rest of your life put up with whatever situation you find yourself in because you're too helpless and hopeless in equal measures to be able to do anything else.'

Every Sikh Punjabi woman that I knew talked about time-passing. Presumably because they had nothing to look forward to, apart from housework, grandchildren and then inevitably death. I always wondered exactly what they were passing time until. Until they died? The downfall of many Sikh Punjabi women was their unequivocal acceptance that life and situations that they found themselves in should be treated as time-passing. Only seeing life as something that has to be endured and survived, they failed to see life as an opportunity to learn, have fun and explore the world.

'How did it feel to be referred to as a burden? It mustn't have been very easy to hear that from your mother.'

'Even though I heard it all the time while I was growing up, it still made me feel awful every time. I couldn't undo my own birth and I felt like I had no right to be here, to be alive and be taking up space on this earth. After we moved to Walsall and I couldn't hear my grandfather criticising the fact that my parents had daughters, my mother's complaints filled the silence. Thanks to her, we became

known in the neighbourhood as the house with the six daughters.'

'It sounds as if your mother was tactless and insensitive to say the least, Jas.'

'Tactless and insensitive doesn't even begin to cover it. She'd say we were a burden, but actually we cooked and cleaned. We used to help our dad if he was fixing the car, passing him spanners and wrenches, helping him change the occasional tyre, holding the ladder for him if he was cleaning the gutters and all sorts of other stuff. When my dad bought an ice-cream van, we'd go with him on his rounds on the weekends and during the school holidays. There were no food or toilet breaks and we'd be on the road with him for hours during the summer. You could have six lazy, drunk, druggie, good-for-nothing sons or six hard-working daughters, but the lazy good-for-nothing sons would still be considered more of a prize because having daughters isn't something to be celebrated in my culture. A lot of Sikh Punjabis can't and won't see any kind of different life for their daughters beyond a married one.'

Twenty-Seven

Flickered

'I want someone who's taller than me,' said Dimple.

Manny laughed. 'I want someone who's really good-looking.'

Sitting on the settee in the living room, my sister and my cousin Manny flicked their hair as they giggled together.

In a corner of the room, I smiled to myself as I turned the page of my book. I already knew who I was going to be with. Lost in my daydreams, I was humming softly to myself when I heard someone calling my name.

'Oi Jas...Jas!'

'Huh?' I glanced across at Dimple and Manny.

'What kind of guy do you wanna marry?' asked Manny.

I stared at her for a second, caught on the back foot, I wasn't sure how to answer. Imagine all the trouble I'd get into if I told my sister and cousin the truth! And just in case they could read my thoughts, quickly I slammed my book shut and jumped to my feet.

'I won't be getting married! I'm going to be a journalist remember?' And with that, I hurried out of the room.

'What you running off for?' Manny called after me.

'Just ignore her, she's stupid! Everyone gets married!' said Dimple, loud enough for me to hear as I headed outside.

There was a high wall at the back of our garden and putting my book down on top of the wall, I pulled myself up next to it and sat down.

Feeling defeated and burdened, I sighed heavily. I seldom resented the gift that I'd been born with, but I always resented it when it came to him - a white Englishman who flickered in my intuition. His name, his face and where he was, I didn't know. All I knew was that the thought of him brought me an incredible sense of joy and contentment. But the sensible and practical part of me would feel distress . . . why was my intuition pulling me towards someone who was impossible?

From where and how could I have gotten the notion that I belonged with an Englishman? I scolded myself. Clearly I'd been reading too many romantic novels, but I wasn't prone to foolishness – my Indian world and his world would not mix. I would never fit into the life and family of a white Englishman nor would he fit into mine. I'd never even had any meaningful interactions with any white people outside of school. The gap from where I stood as a child of poverty-stricken Punjabi immigrants to this Englishman was too wide for me to cross.

Though I'd silently ridicule Dimple and Manny for their love of gossip and the absurd number of hours that they'd spend trying out different hairstyles, rolling my eyes whenever they talked about what their future husbands would be like, occasionally a small part of me envied them.

It took a certain type of person to be content to have their future decided for them. Every other girl I knew, like Dimple and Manny, seemed happy to quietly go and have an arranged marriage, content to put themselves into a box and close the lid. I'd never heard Dimple or Manny mention that they had any other ambition, apart from becoming someone's wife.

Maybe they were keen on getting married because they were constantly being told that life only begins after marriage. All of our parents always told us the same thing: that we could do whatever we wanted after we got married. Once married, we would be allowed to do all of the things that we weren't allowed to do as young, single girls. We weren't allowed to cut our hair, shave our legs, wear makeup or go out by ourselves. It was made very clear that we could only do all of these things after we got married. But what our parents didn't tell us was that after a girl is married, her parents hand over control of her to her husband and his family and they'd pick up the reins and usually hold them even tighter. The idea that a life of freedom awaited us after marriage was an illusion. I was already beginning to understand that, but most girls would never think to look any deeper or beyond what they were told by their families. They would never look to the world outside - a world full of different people with different lives. Marriage would happen to all of us girls, I knew that much. But it would never happen to me, not until I'd become a journalist and fulfilled all of my dreams of experiencing a world outside of my family and relatives.

I sighed. Why couldn't I be more like my sister and cousin? When I already knew my place in the eyes of my family, the Sikh community and the white boys at school. When I wasn't good enough for any of them, I certainly wasn't going to be good enough for any Englishman.

I tried to dismiss all thoughts of him as I stood up and walked along the top of the wall. Feeling a light breeze on my face, I turned my head and looked up at the clear blue sky. The sky looked so beautiful that I caught my breath and instinctively I felt a strong pull towards him. Unsettled and hoping that he would leave, I jumped down from the wall. I landed hard, but he remained. Quiet, unrelenting and steady, like a faithful lighthouse that beams out across dark, stormy waters.

'Over the years I've succeeded in ignoring it. Dismissing the feeling as some silly schoolgirl notion, but it's still there. I feel like it mocks me now and I get really annoyed because I still don't know where he is. I know he's out there, but I'm fucking fed up! And I hate him, whoever he is and wherever he is, I hate him!'

'But how can you hate someone who you don't even know Jas? You've never met him.'

'I know! But that's why I hate him - because he's not here, as stupid and as unreasonable as that sounds. And then I think to myself why do I even care? He'll just be a loser and an asshole like all of the other men that I know!'

'Maybe this man isn't a loser or an asshole. Maybe that's why he's remained with you.'

I rolled my eyes. 'I don't know why I even care. It's not like I've ever tried to find him. The only thing I know is that these feelings of intuition that I have, that I can never explain, that have no rhyme or reason to them, as random and as remote as they are, are always right.'

Twenty-Eight

Flowers Or Sweets

'I'm not wrong Jas! I'm telling you! I'm not wrong!' Devinder said as she grabbed my arm and tried to hold me back.

I shook her off. 'Well, I think you are! I'm gonna go and ask 'em!'

I'd started secondary school at Alumwell Comprehensive. The school was spread across two separate sites, lower school and the main school building, which we referred to as 'big school.' Big school was along the same stretch of road, Primley Avenue as the Alumwell Infant and Junior schools. It had an indoor heated swimming pool, football fields, tennis courts, a fully equipped 100-seat drama theatre and a sports hall with a climbing wall along one side. In contrast, lower school was an old Victorian building, with long tiled corridors and wooden desks with inkwells. Lower school was a five-minute walk from my house if I cut across the grounds of Manor Hospital. The hospital had a large and open grassy area in the middle of all the buildings and my sisters and I would use that as a shortcut to get to school, crossing carefully in case we came upon the security guards who patrolled the grounds of the hospital.

At junior school, I'd been among only a handful of brown children, but after I'd started at Alumwell Comprehensive, I realised that Walsall was full of children like me. During my first week at school, I'd already made friends with Devinder, a Sikh girl and Maria, a black girl.

During one of the morning break-times, I had noticed that Devinder was glaring at a group of girls who had wandered across to us. I didn't know what Devinder said to them, but the girls had quietly left and retreated to the other side of the playground. I asked Devinder what was wrong and why she didn't want them to join us. She turned to me and pulled a face. 'They're Muslims.'

'Muslims?' I scoffed at Devinder. 'Don't you pay any attention at the gurdwara?!' Having spent most of my childhood with my nose buried in books, confined to only being around my family and the Sikh community, I didn't believe that those girls were Muslims. I knew from the recitals at the gurdwara that there had been lots of big battles between Sikhs and Muslims and all the Muslims had been killed. So if all the Muslims had been killed in battles long ago, then the girls who were standing in a school playground in Walsall couldn't possibly be Muslims, could they?

'Fine!' Devinder stopped trying to grab me. 'If you think you're so clever Jas, go on then! Go and ask 'em if you don't believe me!'

'Fine! I will!' I turned and walked across the playground towards the group of girls.

I approached the girls with a curious smile. 'Alright, I'm Jas.'

As they all smiled back at me, I relaxed. They seemed to be just like me, these friendly girls couldn't possibly be Muslims.

'Alright.' Grinned one of the girls.

'Hi, I'm Sadia,' said another.

I noticed that they were all wearing long skirts over their trousers. It looked odd and since there was no easy way to ask the girls the question that I really wanted to ask, I went for a different approach. 'Why you guys wearing trousers and skirts?'

'It's so we're covered up properly,' said Sadia.

Sikh women had to cover up too, especially when they were in the gurdwara so I understood that, but at school my sisters and I wore skirts.

I edged closer to Sadia. 'You have to cover up even at school? Why's that?'

Sadia shrugged. 'It's what our mum and dad tell us to do because it's in our religion.'

'Oh . . . what religion are you?' I asked, holding my breath.

'Muslim,' said Sadia.

'We're all Muslims,' added another girl. I would later find out her name was Roshna.

I tried not to show that I was shocked. 'Oh. Ok.'

Now that I knew what to look for, I glanced around the playground to see if I could spot any boys who were Muslim. I could see that there were quite a few Muslim girls in the playground, but I couldn't tell the Muslim boys apart from the rest of the brown faces.

Puzzled I turned back to the girls. 'Are there any Muslim boys at our school? Do they have to cover up too?'

At my questions, some of the girls laughed out loud. 'There's lots and lots of Muslim boys at school! But they don't have to cover up! It's just us girls,' said Sadia.

I frowned, I didn't think it was funny at all. 'But why is it just girls?'

Sadia scoffed. 'Because that's just the way it is! It's so that nobody else can see the shape of our bodies. Then after we get married, it means that only our husband will have seen us, only he's allowed to look at our bodies.'

Confused and unable to stop myself, I giggled. 'Do you lot have something special on your bodies then, that all the men in the world will stop what they're doing and look at you?!'

Bewildered, the girls stared at me.

'No,' said Roshna. 'It's just our religion, isn't it!'

Her voice hard, Sadia piped in. 'We're just like flowers waiting to open, like sweets all wrapped up.'

Her steely tone made me chuckle even more. 'But you're not flowers or sweets, are you?! You're girls . . . humans . . . the same as boys.'

Sadia only shrugged as the rest of the girls began to look uneasy.

I couldn't understand why these girls were ready to believe that God - who'd taken the trouble to create everything, the earth, the moon, the sun, the stars, the trees, the seas, the mountains, the rivers and all the millions of creatures - would then want women to cover up. If God really had been that bothered, he would have factored it in at the point of creation.

Feeling a sudden rush of sympathy for the girls, I stopped laughing. 'Hey do you guys wanna do handstands? We can go around to the back of the canteen.'

Two of the girls stepped forward as the others shook their heads, saying they'd watch. As I started to walk towards the canteen with my new friends, Devinder hurried across the playground to me.

She sucked in her breath. 'Come on Jas, let's go.'

I shook my head. 'I'm gonna play with these lot. We're going round to the back of the canteen to do handstands. You wanna come with us?'

'No thanks!' Devinder snorted and shooting me a look, she marched off.

I shrugged and walked around the corner to do handstands with the very ordinary and sweet enemies of Sikhs.

'Considering that I grew up watching Bollywood movies, no one in my family ever explained that some of the characters being portrayed were Muslims. I just thought people in India dressed in different costumes and I was so surprised, shocked even, to find out that my new friends all lived just down the road with lots of other Muslims. I did find the girls' quiet acceptance of religious beliefs odd though. In Sikhism men and women are to be treated as equals and no one should impose their will onto another person. Of course the reality is that some Sikh men are selective about which parts of the Guru Granth Sahib they actually pay attention to - from my experience only the parts that suit their egos. If Muslim men had to cover up too, then it's equal, then it's fair. I think people either have the ability to see inequality and fight it or they just accept what they're told without questioning or thinking for themselves. If men can't control women by using social and cultural expectations, that men invented in the first place, then they'll bring out the big guns - they'll use religion . . . which men also invented. Cos let's face it . . . if you're scared of going to hell and you wanna please God, then you'll do whatever you're told to do regardless of whether it feels right, good or makes your life unequal to that of a man's.'

'I can see how any form of inequality would annoy you Jas.'

'The older I got, the more I realised that I was surrounded by inequality everywhere. There was a massive divide and rivalry between Sikhs and Muslims at my school, but I tried not to get dragged into it. The Sikhs at my school treated the Muslims as inferior and I was in the minority of Sikhs who were friendly with the Muslims. As soon as I settled into secondary school, I was told by my parents that one of the worst things that a Sikh girl could do was to be friends with any Muslim boys. While I already knew that I

wasn't allowed to talk to any boys, my parents made it very clear that talking to Muslim boys was worse than anything else a girl could do. Friendships between Sikh and Muslim girls was frowned upon and discouraged, but according to my family and the wider Sikh Punjabi community, there was no greater horror or dishonour that a girl could bestow upon her family than befriending Muslim boys.'

Twenty-Nine

A Storm Is Coming

'What do your sisters think they're doing?' My mother asked my dad, leaning closer to him as they both stood in the kitchen. 'Yesterday I saw Pally and Navi getting into a car full of Muslim boys! And last week one of the neighbours saw them getting into a car as well!'

Standing at the sink, I kept my head down as I washed up the breakfast dishes.

My mother huffed. 'They're getting into cars and being driven off to God knows where! To do God knows what! Your father needs to do something!'

My dad shifted uncomfortably. Mumbling that he'd speak to my mother about it later, he left the kitchen.

One of our neighbours had spotted my aunts Pally and Navi climbing into a car full of boys - Muslim boys. Not bold enough to inform my dad, the neighbor had rushed over to tell my mother instead. No sooner had my mother dismissed what she'd heard as malicious gossip, when a few days later she'd seen for herself, Pally and Navi getting into a car. My mother had hurried across to the car, but it had sped off with both girls inside. After seeing what she'd seen, my mother had had no choice, but to tell my dad - not telling him would mean my mother was complicit with what Pally and Navi were doing.

Later that afternoon, my mother sat talking with the neighbour who'd seen my two aunts getting into the car. 'My father-in-law walks both of them to and from school and they've been complaining about it, but no one is taking their side anymore! How can anyone take their side? They're leaving school during the middle of the day...what's their father supposed to do? Sit outside the school all day and watch who stays and who goes! Where are they going with those boys? And why are they going? Do they think that people outside of our family don't know? Of course they know! Before we find out what's going on with our daughters and sisters, the rest of the world already has the full picture of who's going where, with who and to do what!'

Tutting loudly, the neighbour nodded. 'Ah that's very true. The outside world knows everything about other people's daughters and what they're doing outside of the house.'

My mother shook her head. 'You know they wanted to wear skirts. I took their side, I even argued against all the men of the house! And because I took their side, they got to wear skirts, but now look at this! Look what they're doing! They're shaving their dad's nose right off and he can't do anything about it! I've told my husband that he and his father and brothers somehow need to sort this out. Everyone will say Daljit can't control his own sisters! When we have eyes and we can see that a storm is coming, then why continue to sit and do nothing! The men want to get both girls married off as soon as possible. That'll bring an end to all of this!'

'Yes, it's better to get them married off before anything else happens or one of them runs away,' said the neighbour.

'The men have already started looking,' said my mother.

She glanced across at me and my sisters as we sat on the living room floor doing our homework. 'I've told my girls a thousand times that they're never to get into a car with boys. If any of them ever do, then they should think of that as the exact moment that they've killed their poor father with their own hands because he'll die from the shame and dishonour. And they don't want to kill their own father, do they? That's what I've told all of them . . . haven't I, girls?'

Silently we all bobbed our heads.

After I started at Alumwell Comprehensive, I'd noticed cars patrolling like sharks, back and forth, up and down Primley Avenue. The cars would slow down in front of my school and idly wait for any opportunity to lure in an impressionable schoolgirl. If no schoolgirl was forthcoming, the cars would set off down the road, predictably circling back a few minutes later to try again. I never saw any white faces in the cars, only brown. Staring out from the open windows of their cars with their arrogant smirks and hollow dark eyes, greedily scouring the pavements for girls. My mother needn't have warned me. Just the mere thought of getting into a car full of boys instinctively churned my stomach.

A few weeks after my mother's conversation with the neighbour, my parents had some news.

'Pally's marriage has been fixed. She'll be married as soon as we can agree a date with the groom's family. We'll book Willenhall gurdwara for the wedding ceremony. Once we've bid her goodbye, we can all start to sleep easier at night!'

'In my family, marriage was seen as the solution to every problem and Pally was married as soon as she turned sixteen. In my grandfather's family, the tradition was that the men of the house find the groom and arrange

everything. None of my dad's four sisters were given any choice or say in their future husbands. The girl is expected to quietly show up on her wedding day and thereinafter keep her mouth permanently shut.'

'Everyone thought that once Pally had been married off, all that stuff with the boys in the cars would be over because Pally was loud and confident and Navi was the quiet one who followed her sister around everywhere. But with Pally gone, Navi became more isolated and alone. We didn't see her much. She was kept away from us by my grandfather and by her brother, my uncle Manjeet. My uncle Manjeet loved being in control and then he turned religious and it was one of the worst things that could ever have happened to our family.'

Thirty

God Was Lost

'Your uncle Manjeet's found God!' Sounding pleased as punch, my mother was beaming.

Surprised I quickly put down my book and jumped to my feet. 'I didn't know God was lost! Where is he now? Can we go and meet him?' I wanted to go and see God before everyone else rushed there too.

My mother turned very red. 'You insolent girl! Why are you so stupid?! Thank goodness no one else can hear the ridiculous things that you say!'

Embarrassed and disappointed, I started to slouch away as my dad walked into the living room. Having overheard my mother, he was chuckling. 'Ah yes Jas, my brother has found God! He's become a fully-fledged Khalsa Sikh and now we'll never get any peace! I know all about these people that find God and then make everyone else's lives unbearable!'

Still red, my mother turned on him. 'You're only worried that you'll have to give up your meat and alcohol!'

Halfway to the front room, I stopped and turned back around. 'Are we gonna have to stop eating meat as well?' I knew that Khalsa Sikhs had to give up alcohol and meat and become vegetarians.

Much to my relief and my mother's annoyance, my dad shook his head. 'I'm not giving up meat and it's not as if I drink all the time. I have one beer every evening and that's all I ask for. Just let me have my one beer in peace.'

'And what about the Jack Daniels you drink in the kitchen after dinner when you think that no one is watching?' muttered my mother.

As my parents began to bicker about my dad's drinking habits, I left them to it.

A couple of days later my uncle Manjeet came to visit. He wore a bright orange turban and across one shoulder and tucked close to his hip he wore a kirpan (a small decorative blade). Known as one of the five K's, my uncle had to wear the blade at all times along with a kach (shorts), kanga (comb), kara (steel bangle) and he wasn't allowed to cut or trim his hair (kesh).

My sisters and I were made to gather round and listen for hours as Manjeet told us that my dad should consider giving up alcohol and meat and we should all consider waking up at the crack of dawn to read holy scriptures before school. We sat and listened quietly as my mother fussed over the first member of our family who had chosen to become a fully-fledged Khalsa Sikh. That evening my dad didn't drink his usual can of beer.

The following evening, my uncle showed up again and talked endlessly about the virtues of Sikhism. As my uncle continued preaching, my dad sat shuffling and shifting his feet around. Finally my dad gave a long and loud sigh, stood up and walked into the kitchen where he opened the fridge and pulled out a can of cold beer.

On the third evening when my uncle Manjeet rang to tell us that he was coming over again, my dad took the telephone from my jabbering mother.

'We're about to eat roast chicken and you'll only spoil it with your lectures. On top of which, the girls are tired from the last two evenings and they have their homework to do. And you already know that I'm not interested.' My dad hung up the telephone to collective sighs of relief from me and my sisters.

'Is that how you speak to your brother! What if he takes offence?' My mother sounded both relieved and anxious.

My dad shrugged. 'I know my brother, he won't take offence. He's had two evenings and he knows that he's lucky he got those! Look at the way the girls sat and listened to him, not once did they complain. There's not many children who would have done that, so I'm not putting them through another evening of it.'

'Don't use the girls as an excuse! Your brother knows that it's you he's got to try and convince,' said my mother.

'I may drink and eat meat, but I'm alright as I am! Now listen up girls,' said my dad.

Surprised we all looked up from our homework. Unlike my mother, it was rare that my dad made speeches.

'Don't think of doing anything bad to other people and treat others how you want to be treated yourself. If people could just grasp that, then this world would be alright. What I don't get is why all these religious people don't understand this! They start preaching to other people as if they suddenly know better and they start behaving as if they are better than everyone else!'

As my sisters and I nodded at our dad, I silently agreed with him, I knew he was right.

One by one, my uncle caught all of our other relatives too. Trapped they would obediently nod their heads up and down, but once released they'd hurry away muttering under their breaths that one religious person in the family was already one too many. A few weeks later, my grandfather also became a fully-fledged

Sikh and so did my aunt Harjit who had no choice, but to follow in her husband Manjeet's footsteps. Being a woman, she couldn't possibly be allowed to make her own mind up about what kind of life she wanted.

Together husband and wife promptly banned their three children from eating meat, dancing at weddings and parties, listening to music and watching films. My uncle Manjeet controlled everything - what his family wore, what they ate, where they went and who they spoke to. They weren't allowed to do anything apart from spend as much time as was humanly possible at the gurdwara. But while his wife and young children quietly and obediently fell into line behind Manjeet, his sister Navi who lived with them refused.

'We all know religious people Jas and I must admit that it can sometimes be hard to listen to them especially if they have strong and different beliefs from our own, but where does this strong dislike come from for you? What's been your experience of religion?'

'My experience of religion is very different to my experience of God. My experience of religion is that the world would be a much better place without any religions. My uncle Manjeet, who nicknamed me 'Ugly Duckling,' he had always been one of my favourite people, but then he just changed overnight. You mainly get three types of Sikhs: those like my dad and the rest of my family who go to the gurdwara, but also eat meat and drink and they're more easy-going. Then there's the rare type of Khalsa Sikhs who are sweet and humble because they understand the true meaning of Sikhism. Along with meat and alcohol they've also given up their egos and they don't shove their religious views or opinions down anyone's throat. Why not? Because they have nothing to prove about God, they're so secure within themselves and the world around them that they're the best kind of person you could ever meet. And then you get the third kind of Sikhs. The Khalsa Sikhs, like my uncle Manjeet, who use religion as an excuse to control their

families and they suck all the fun and joy out of living. They have to show off their devotion to God by referring to him morning, noon and night, making everyone around them miserable and life void of fun and light. My uncle was already a controlling person, but after he became religious, he thought he was superior to everyone else. Most of the religious people that I know have zero understanding about the value of life and yet they claim to know all about what God wants. Don't make me laugh - with their big egos getting in the way, they can't even see God, let alone know what he wants!'

Thirty-One

Red With A Hint Of Purple

'I can call him if that's what he wants, but I don't know what to say or do,' mumbled my dad. He turned to my mother. 'Are you quite sure of what he said? He thinks he's seen him?'

Sitting at her sewing machine, my mother's tone was short. 'When your brother called, all he told me was that he's sure that a boy is coming into the house late at night after everyone has gone to bed.'

My dad pondered out loud. 'But how can someone get into the house if it's all locked up?'

'Well . . . he's not a ghost who's able to come in through locked doors and windows now, is he?! Someone must be letting him into the house,' said my mother. 'What other explanation can there be? Why don't you just call Manjeet and speak to him yourself?'

Sighing my dad shuffled his feet as both my parents fell into a heavy silence. Sitting quietly in a corner of the living room, I turned the page of my book, *The Outsiders*. I'd never heard my parents sound so strained before, not even when they'd faced legal challenges trying to get my masi British citizenship.

Eventually my mother broke the silence. 'Pally was married off and we should have got Navi married off at the same time too because what's happening now is very bad, it's very bad indeed.'

'You already know that in this country we can't just marry off our girls!' snapped my dad. 'We have to wait until they turn sixteen! Otherwise we'd have already got Navi married off and finished the job!'

Turning away, my mother switched on her sewing machine and reached for the pieces of material beside her. But before she put her head down, she turned back to my dad. 'Just call your brother tonight when he gets home from work . . . what else can you do?'

'In India if a girl plays with her family's honour and tries to cut off her family's nose, her throat is cut and she's tossed into the nearest river!' Clearing his throat, my dad's face began to turn red with anger. 'She'd be cut into a thousand tiny pieces and thrown into the water and the currents would carry the pieces away and no one would know and no one would find out and no one would care! Everyone would just carry on, as if nothing had ever happened. They're dead, they're gone, good riddance, job done! And no one would ever mention the name of the dead again!'

As my dad left the room, muttering about the benefits of strong river currents, I'd listened with growing fury at the mention of honour. A stupid notion made up by men so that they could control their sisters, daughters and wives, it hung like an invisible chain around the throats of Indian women. 'Don't do this and don't do that because you'll embarrass your father!' I knew the concept of honour was only about fragile men with big egos who were scared of being embarrassed in front of their neighbours and community. The colour of honour was red with a hint of purple which also happens to be the colour of most men's faces when they're embarrassed and they get all puffed up like idiots.

'So from a young age Jas, ideas about honour were placed into your head by your family?'

'Yep. All the time.'

'To control you?'

'Yes. Told to us so we would hear and heed the horror stories that never ended well for the girl involved. These things were deliberately discussed loudly and openly in our house so that we would heed the warnings about the consequences of bringing shame onto our family because no girl wants to end up being cut into a thousand pieces and thrown into a river. These sorts of examples were constantly fed to us, but I could see the inequality in the idea of honour. It's ridiculous that the whole of your family's honour, whatever that means, is placed exclusively on the shoulders of girls and used to control their behaviour. For girls it's honour and shame and for boys they can do whatever they want, with whoever they want and it's ok . . . though occasionally something goes wrong, very wrong for a boy too.'

Thirty-Two

One Of Ours

'Please mum...please?' pleaded Dimple.

'Can we go mum?' begged Sarb.

'Why are you making such a fuss? Let the girls go with me,' said my dad.

My mother, having never previously stopped us before, was suddenly adamant that she didn't want me and my sisters to visit Navi and our young cousins in Bentley.

Standing silently beside Dimple, Sarb and my dad, I didn't need to add my voice. I knew if Dimple and my dad both wanted something their way, my mother would eventually cave. And after much persuasion, she did so reluctantly, but she had a condition – we all had to return back home in the evening with our dad.

'You're not to stay there overnight! Do you understand? All of you have to return home with your dad! Now promise me girls you'll all return home tonight!'

My mother had never made us promise anything before and its strangeness stuck in my head. Dimple,

Sarb and I quickly made the necessary promise and left with my dad.

We enjoyed being back in our childhood home and time flew as we spent the entire day playing with Navi and our younger cousins, Banita, Sweety and Tandip.

Later that evening my dad called me and my sisters to him. 'Girls, it's time to go home.'

To my surprise, Dimple and Sarb started begging my dad to let them stay the night, both of them refusing to leave.

My dad glanced at me. 'Jas, do you want to stay here as well?'

I knew that if my sisters were going to disobey our mother, I could too. From past experience, I knew that the more of us who disobeyed my mother, the more diluted our punishment. Torn between breaking a promise and wanting to stay, I hesitated for a moment. And in that moment, just at my elbow, I felt the presence of my grandmother Mama. And just like a recording, clear as a bell, I heard my mother's voice - 'you're not to stay there overnight! Do you understand? All of you have to return home with your dad! Now promise me girls you'll all return home tonight!'

And I knew, without any doubt that I should heed my mother's words. I could have more fun if I stayed, but I shook my head. 'I don't wanna stay dad. I'll go home with you.'

'Are you sure? You don't need to worry about getting into trouble with your mum. Sometimes she makes a lot of noise about nothing!'

I was so sure that I didn't even take the time to say goodbye to anyone properly as I quickly climbed into my dad's car. I was disappointed to miss out on having even more fun with my cousins and Navi, but returning home still felt like it was the right thing to do. Though I couldn't quite put my finger on why.

When my dad returned home with only me in tow, my mother hit the roof. She was so angry and worried that she made my dad promise he'd return to Bentley first thing in the morning to collect Dimple and Sarb.

'Why do you worry?' asked my dad. 'When I'm not worried, why are you? I think you're just looking for any excuse to have an argument with me! I haven't left them in some strange place, have I? They're staying in their uncle's house! Goodness woman, why do you make such a fuss about things! I'll go and collect them first thing in the morning!'

Despite my dad promising to return to Bentley early the next morning to collect my sisters, my mother was still furious. 'Why did you leave them there in the first place when I told you not to? I may be just a woman, but if anything happens, you're going to be the one who's going to regret leaving them! Especially when I told you not to!'

I couldn't understand my mother's over-reaction, yet as I drifted off to sleep that night, I felt relieved to be in my own bed.

Past midnight, the sound of the telephone ringing downstairs woke me up, but tired I drifted back to sleep.

Early the next morning, I woke to the sound of the telephone ringing off the hook and a terrible wailing that randomly stopped and started. I slowly walked downstairs and into the living room. It was jam-packed with relatives and neighbours. As I quietly brushed past people and made my way through to the kitchen towards the bathroom, I heard snippets and snatches of conversations.

'It beggars belief that a Muslim can think it's a good idea to enter a Sikh man's house in the middle of the night!'

'Anyone who's a Sikh, Hindu or a Muslim will know that when you're seeing someone from a different religion, there's going to be trouble. Why didn't this boy know?'

'Trouble? Of course yes! But this kind of trouble?'

'Why didn't he just run?'

'That poor boy's mother. It's so terrible! What must she be going through this morning?'

'He used the window to try to escape, but-'

'Escape? How could a nineteen year old boy who spent all of his time driving around picking up schoolgirls be a match for someone who's worked in foundries all of his life? It couldn't have been much of a fight!'

'It's such an awful thing!'

'How could he not have known how Sikhs and Muslims are towards each other?'

'Maybe he did know . . . but obviously he didn't care.'

'When Manjeet woke up, he heard something. So he got up to check and that's when he caught the Muslim climbing out of one of the bedroom windows.'

'Manjeet should have just given the boy a good hiding and then let him go! This is so awful I don't even want to think about it!'

'No one says you have to take someone's life just because!'

'What must his poor mother be going through today? All mothers feel the same pain, no matter which God they worship.'

I couldn't believe what I was hearing. Using his kirpan, my uncle Manjeet had stabbed a nineteen year old boy called Kabir and killed him.

Watching from the window of the girls' bedroom, Navi, Dimple and Sarb had seen the entire struggle unfold in the front garden as Kabir had desperately tried to escape my uncle's grip. He had eventually managed to wriggle free and stagger away, but he'd already been stabbed.

My uncle had returned inside and rang my dad to let him know what had happened. But at the time what my uncle didn't know, was that Kabir had only made it a few yards down the road before he'd collapsed. He had died on the pavement and was found in the early hours of Monday morning. The police dogs traced the scent straight back to Manjeet's house and my uncle had been arrested.

When Dimple and Sarb returned home later that morning, not a single person asked them how they were. To this day, they both remain traumatized by what they witnessed. Dimple has never spoken of that night and if anyone ever mentions the incident to her, even in passing, she just starts sobbing.

'On the day of Kabir's funeral, my dad sat quietly in our front room. He went down to the solicitors every day, sometimes twice a day to try and help with my uncle's case, but that day he didn't go anywhere. We all knew that somewhere in Walsall, there was a house filled with grief, but we couldn't do anything to help them. We couldn't even go and say sorry because it was one of ours who had caused them that pain in the first place.'

'How did it feel knowing that you couldn't express your condolences to Kabir's family?'

'I just felt useless. And as if the divisions between Sikhs and Muslims had widened beyond repair and would never come to an end. Maybe Kabir's family thought we were ok with what had happened to them. But they'll never know how terrible we felt. While my uncle would return after a few years in prison, they'd lost their son forever.' I sighed.

'That was a very heavy sigh Jas.'

I looked out of the window. 'I was just thinking about how when my uncle found God and then he found Kabir climbing out of the bedroom window, those two events altered the course of our family history. Us girls already had a small, closed-off existence, but after Kabir's death, the noose around our necks became tighter. We were watched and monitored every minute of every day by an adult. We weren't even allowed to go and play in the garden without an adult being present. And our teachers were told about what had happened and asked to keep an eye on us. And even though we were old enough to walk there by ourselves, we were escorted to and from school by a member of our family every day for a couple of years afterwards. Some of that was in case Kabir's family tried to retaliate, but I think it was mostly just an excuse to watch and control the rest of us girls even more. Once one girl goes awry, inevitably the noose gets tighter around the necks of the other girls in the family.'

Thirty-Three

Irony And Karma

'Move over!'

'You move over, you idiot!'

As another argument broke out between my cousin Sweety and my sister Pardeep about sharing the space on the double bed, I turned away and pulled the covers over my head. But with my cousin and my sister arguing and a constant hum of voices drifting up from downstairs, it was impossible for me to get back to sleep.

After Manjeet had been taken to prison, his wife Harjit stated that she didn't feel safe in her own home, insisting that someone had to stay with her overnight. So the adults decided that my sisters and I would take turns sleeping over at the house. But Dimple refused point-blank - she didn't ever want to go back there – so because I was the second eldest, my parents decided that I should go with my younger sisters as companions.

But I hated staying there. After Kabir's death, the house never felt the same again. It was gloomy and tainted, no longer the place where some of my favourite childhood memories had been made. At night, my grandfather would take his sleeping pills and be oblivious to the world while my aunt Harjit would barricade herself into her bedroom with her son Tandip, leaving me and my sisters with her two daughters Banita and Sweety to fend for ourselves next door in the girls' bedroom, which had no lock on the door.

A few months into the new sleeping arrangement, around 3am one morning, things came to a head. My sister Bina who was sleeping next to Sarb, woke up and was violently sick in Sarb's hair. Amid Sarb's screeching, in the ensuing darkness and chaos, I was abruptly awakened and forced to step in and physically hold Sarb back to prevent her from beating Bina to a pulp. During the fracas, while I was performing the unenviable task of trying to comb the sick out of Sarb's hair, Harjit opened her bedroom door and shouted at us for waking her up.

We returned back home in the morning and after relaying the night's events to my parents, they realised that Harjit was locking herself in her bedroom, leaving me to deal with any problems that arose during the night. My dad suggested that my grandfather, Harjit and her three children move in with us instead. Apart from Harjit, everyone else agreed that it was the right decision.

For the next three years, nine children and five adults lived together in our three-bed, one bathroom mid terrace house. During the day, we were forced to share every bit of space and at night we slept four to a bed. Space and quietness quickly became a thing of the past. Harjit, unwilling to remain by herself in her own home, but furious that she had to move in with us, created a variety of problems from the very first day that she moved in.

Harjit's sister and numerous other relatives of hers lived in Coventry, but not a single one of them offered her any sanctuary or any other kind of help while her husband was in prison. Nonetheless, they turned up en masse on our doorstep to complain about my parents' treatment of Harjit.

My dad, sometimes known to demonstrate the patience of a saint, watched as we quietly served Harjit's relatives tea and biscuits. He listened silently to all of their criticisms and snide comments about his tiny house and his family before he asked them all one question. 'Harjit is having such an awful time living in Walsall, but as far as we are concerned she's free to leave and live elsewhere any time she wants. So do any of you want to take her and her three children to stay with you?' With a deafening silence filling the room, my dad quietly got to his feet and politely bid them farewell.

My aunt Harjit had changed the moment her husband had been arrested. Making no secret of the fact that she hated her father-in-law, Harjit refused to speak to my grandfather unless it was to argue with him. She believed that her husband would not have ended up in prison if my grandfather had dealt with Navi differently. Waiting until my dad was out of the house and then no longer quiet and polite, like she used to be, she would shout and scream at my grandfather for hours on end. My grandfather could usually hold his own against her, but the verbal onslaught from Harjit was so relentless, that at times even he seemed dazed and bewildered. She made his every waking moment into a confrontation. Between the two of them arguing day and night because we all had to share such a small space, they made everyone else's lives unbearable too.

The shock of one of his sons being sent to prison had weakened my grandfather. Since all of the beds were taken, he'd been left with no choice, but to sleep downstairs on one of the settees. On top of which, citing religious reasons, my uncle Manjeet refused to eat the prison food so every day my grandfather would have to wait for Harjit to cook Manjeet's food and then he'd have to travel on several buses to get to the prison in Birmingham to deliver Manjeet's food.

Having become Khalsa Sikhs along with Manjeet, my grandfather and my aunt Harjit were both vegetarians, which meant two different meals would have to be cooked every evening. My aunt resented cooking for my grandfather and would serve him the same several days old dal again and again while she made fresh meals for herself and her three children. While our dinner would be served to us by my mother hot and without any fuss, my grandfather's dinner would be served to him by Harjit deliberately cold with an extra dollop of shouting.

'That's not the image of your grandfather that you were used to seeing, were you?'

'No, not at all. When some people are younger and stronger they behave terribly towards their children and daughter-in-law, but as they age, they become fragile and vulnerable. Then they have to rely on the very people that they used to abuse to look after them and pray that the person caring for them isn't holding a grudge. Years earlier, my grandfather had kicked us out because he was riding high on his other three sons, but my uncle Sandeep left for Australia, my uncle Taran went to live in Birmingham with his new wife and my uncle Manjeet went to prison. Out of my grandfather's four sons, the only son who didn't desert him was my dad - that's irony and karma in motion.'

Thirty-Four

My Mother's Mother

'Do you lot know who's coming to our house tomorrow?' asked my mother.

Silently praying that it wasn't one of our horrid cousins or some boring relative, my sisters and I braced ourselves.

'My mother! My mother is coming from India tomorrow! And my younger brother Joshan is arriving two days after her! Isn't that wonderful?' My mother was practically squealing with delight. 'They're both going to live here with us. I didn't think they'd ever be able to come, but I've managed to swing it!' My mother was beaming from ear to ear.

We all stared at her in stunned silence. I was so used to being around my dad's family that it had never occurred to me that besides masi and her two brothers and her sister who had died in India, that my mother may have more family members, let alone a mother of her own! I couldn't even begin to imagine my mother as someone's daughter, someone's little girl. It hadn't ever occurred to me that there was anything else to my mother, apart from being my mother.

I frowned. 'You have a mother? A real one?'

'How come you have a mother and you didn't tell us before?' asked Sarb.

My mother's smile vanished. 'Really! Do you girls think I dropped from the sky? Of course I have a mother! Dimple has met her, she'll tell you!' She turned to shout in the direction of the kitchen. 'Dimple! Dimple! Come here and tell your stupid sisters all about Bibi!'

Wiping her hands on a tea-towel, Dimple hurried in. 'What's the matter?'

My mother bobbed her head. 'Tell your sisters about Bibi.'

'Bibi? What do you want me to say about her?' Dimple threw her head back and grinned. 'Let them see for themselves what she's like when she gets here!'

My mother laughed. As she worked out the sleeping arrangements, she couldn't stop smiling. She'd been a young woman when she'd first moved to England and married my dad. Leaving everything, including her family behind, my mother had had to adapt to a new country and a new family. My mother told me and my sisters that lots of Indian women who left India and married abroad, never saw their parents again. Once a girl was married, it was up to her husband and his family whether she was ever allowed to return home. Various reasons would be cited by her in-laws for their refusal, such as how would they manage without their daughter-in-law to cook and clean for them, they didn't have the money to send her home or that it was simply not-the-right-time. By the time the in-laws died and these women gained some freedom, their own parents may also have died - just like my mother's father had.

Once Bibi and my uncle Joshan arrived, there would be nine children and seven adults in our house. Usually it's relatives of the husband who live with his family, I didn't know anyone else whose maternal grandmother and mother's brother lived with them.

Brimming with happiness, my mother set us all to work, cleaning and tidying, while my masi and Harjit cooked up a feast in the kitchen.

'Shall we play a trick on Bibi?' I whispered to my sisters. Eagerly they nodded as I told them my plan. With my sisters on board, I asked permission from my parents.

My dad laughed. 'Ok, but don't end up giving the old woman a heart attack!'

'We won't,' I promised.

The morning Bibi was due to arrive from India, my sisters and I all sprang out of bed. We spent most of the day waiting impatiently for my dad and uncle to collect her from the airport.

'Dad's back! They're here!' Sarb finally shouted. Sitting in the window of the front room watching the road through the net curtains, she was on look-out duty.

Scrambling around my sisters and cousins, I watched with bated breath to catch the first glimpse of my mother's mother. In the back of my mind, I wouldn't quite believe it until I saw her for myself.

Unaccustomed to cars, Bibi emerged somewhat awkwardly from the back seat. Arriving in the middle of a cold October, she pulled her scarf and coat tightly around herself as she left the car. Bibi was very tall and thin with a long slender body and impossibly long arms and legs. My dad had parked the car on double yellow lines, right up at the front door. The pavement outside our front door was so narrow that Bibi would only need to take one step with her long legs and she would be standing in the front room.

My grandmother's wrinkled and weathered face wore a bemused and somewhat bewildered look as she glanced around at her new surroundings. Slowly her eyes travelled from one person to the next as one-by-one she surveyed her daughter's daughters.

'Hello Bibi!'

'Hi!'

'How are you Bibi?'

'Hello!'

A chorus of greetings echoed throughout the room and it seemed to take Bibi forever to give everyone the customary hugs before she cautiously sat down on one of the settees.

Tea and food were promptly placed in front of my grandmother and my mother who was almost beside herself with happiness, chatting non-stop.

But we began to get impatient. We wanted to pull our prank, but until my mother suggested that Bibi go upstairs for a rest, we wouldn't be able to put my plan into action. It was only after we all began to shift and fidget that my mother could no longer ignore us and so she asked Bibi to go upstairs and take a nap to recover from her long flight.

I immediately jumped up. 'Here Bibi, I'll take you upstairs and show you where you're going to be sleeping.'

I opened the door that lead to the stairs and then stepped back so Bibi could go upstairs first. She stepped forward into the dimly lit narrow stairway and immediately screamed and jumped back.

'Oh! What's this baby doing here? Whose baby is this?' Looking horrified, Bibi screeched as she peered into the stairway. 'Why have you left a baby lying on the stairs like this? How can you be so careless? Oh my goodness, what if it falls? One of you quickly come here and pick up this baby! Oh my goodness. Oh dear! Hurry now! One of you pick it up!'

All around Bibi, we collapsed into laughter.

'Why are you all laughing? Are you crazy? What's wrong with you? Come and pick up this baby before it starts crying! Why are you all just standing around laughing?'

We were all laughing because I'd placed my doll on the stairs in the dimly lit stairway. As Bibi continued screaming, I swooped my doll up by one of its legs and held it upside down.

'Look Bibi!' I swung the doll under Bibi's nose. 'It's only a doll! See?'

For a second I thought my grandmother was going to pass out, but looking bewildered she abruptly stopped screeching. Her open mouth flapped closed as she stood still. Slowly a look of amazement swept across her face as she peered more closely at the doll.

'Oh!' She fell silent for a few moments before she held out one of her long arms. 'Here let me see it.'

I handed her my doll.

Quietly she turned it over in her hands and inspected it from head to toe. 'Wow! Imagine that! What things they make these days! Goodness me! And here I was thinking that it was a real baby!'

'Mum and dad gave it to me for my birthday.'

'Ah.' She pulled her eyes away from my doll and peered at me. 'You're the one younger than Dimple, aren't you?'

I nodded.

'You didn't come to India with them, did you? They should have brought you along with them that time. We'd heard so much about you, we were all waiting for you to come.'

I shrugged. 'I'll go to India when I get big.'

'Who knows when you'll get big,' murmured my grandmother. She glanced down at the doll in her hands. 'Can I keep it for a little while?'

I nodded.

In the days that followed, Bibi mused over my doll, only setting it aside when relatives and neighbours came to visit her.

A few months later, when my mother said I had outgrown my doll and that she was thinking of sending it to India for my younger cousins to play with, I didn't mind. Bibi's arrival and the amazement in her eyes when she had surveyed all the things that we had, made me realise that although we were poor, by no means, were we the poorest.

'How did you feel about your grandmother Jas? I'm just thinking about the attachments you have to both your grandmothers.'

'Mama and Bibi were different to the rest of the adults in my life. Mama was special because she would occasionally return to guide me and I know to have that is a very unique experience and I'm lucky to have the ability to sense her presence. I only wish that she'd visit me more often. Bibi was the only adult in my house who brought any light and joy to my life because she was quite unusual. On the one hand, she was very reserved and refined and she'd worry about what people might say or think of our family. But then on the other hand she'd sit in the garden combing her long hair - she had the longest hair I'd ever seen and she'd just sit there singing loudly without a care in the world. And sometimes she would yell and run around in the garden, laughing and screeching her head off.'

'Maybe that's why she was so fascinated by your doll Jas. Maybe she'd missed out on playing with dolls and running around. Children play and they run around and that's what your grandmother was doing when she came to live with you. Though part of her was an adult and wary of what people would say and think, the child- part of her wanted to be fulfilled too.'

'You're right, Bibi didn't really have a childhood. Like a lot of girls in those days, she wasn't sent to school and she was married off around the age of thirteen, fourteen. So she never got any kind of education nor did she have any time to play because before her parents married her off, she had to do all the chores in the house. Her life had been full of hard work, trauma and extreme poverty.'

Thirty-Five

Bhagat Who?

'Bhagat? Bhagat who?' I screwed my nose up at Bibi. 'Is he one of our relatives from India?'

Bibi didn't answer me. Instead she clasped her hands together in unhappy amazement, throwing a confused gaze at my dad. 'She doesn't know who Bhagat Singh is?'

Avoiding Bibi's stare, my dad took a small intake of breath and cleared his throat. 'No. We haven't told the girls anything.'

Bibi narrowed her eyes and pursed her lips together. My dad was her son-in-law and she was reluctant to have any kind of disagreement with him, but she couldn't help herself. 'I'm amazed that you haven't told them! Why haven't you?'

My dad shrugged. 'They're too young to understand about that kind of thing. Besides it's all in the past now.'

Once more Bibi pressed her lips tightly together. She said nothing, but bobbing her head down, she suddenly appeared to be very interested in picking at some flint on the carpet.

In the strained silence, I understood that in any disagreement, my dad would always win because he was Bibi's son-in-law and sons-in-law were held in such high regard in Sikh Punjabi families, that my dad's views and opinions would always take precedence.

The next morning while both of my parents were running errands in town, I cornered Bibi. 'Tell me who is Bhagat Singh? Is he one of your relatives?'

I believed Bibi would put up a fight and refuse to tell me, so I was surprised when she patted the empty spot next to her on the settee.

'Come here. Sit.'

Bibi cleared her throat and for a second I feared she had changed her mind, but then she leaned in. 'I don't know if your parents are going to approve of me telling you this, but you'll find out some day anyway.' She settled herself into the settee. 'Now listen and listen properly. Bhagat Singh was a Sikh who lived in India when I was just a young girl. My mother and father used to speak about him often, but always in hushed tones, because no one was allowed to talk about Bhagat Singh. The white man wouldn't allow anyone to mention his name and if you got caught, you'd be in trouble.'

I frowned. 'But why would the white man care about anyone in India talking about this Bhagat Singh?'

'Because the white man ruled over India for many hundreds of years. That's why they were worried about Bhagat Singh.'

Feeling a sudden rush of blood to my head, I was glad I was sitting down. I couldn't believe what I'd just heard. 'The white man used to rule India?'

Bibi nodded. 'Yes. I saw for myself everything that the white man did in India and how badly they treated us. It all happened in front of my very eyes. All the terrible, terrible things that they did.'

'But Bibi, why would the white man go to India?'

'There's only fields and cows there.'

Bibi shook her head, her eyes filled with despair at my ignorance. 'Do you know how special the soil and earth is over there? Especially in the Punjab. It has some of the richest fields in the world, where crops and plants grow in abundance. Everyone knows that there's no other soil that can be compared to the soil found in the Punjab, that's why the Punjab is so valuable.'

She sighed. 'The white men first came to India as visitors and traders, but they soon realised the wealth and riches that India had. They bribed the Maharajas, giving them gifts and money in exchange for control over their land. Helped by the greedy Maharajas who didn't care about the poor, the white men gradually managed to take over all of India. They had big guns and bullets, but the poor villagers who lived and worked on the land . . . what did they have? They had nothing to fight back with. Religion already divided the poor anyway - Hindus, Muslims and Sikhs all disliked and mistrusted each other so our own stupidity made it even easier for the white man to get control.'

Trying to get rid of a lump that had suddenly formed in my throat, I swallowed hard.

'The white man ruled with an iron fist and those who got out of line were killed. Bhagat Singh wanted the white man out of India. It wasn't their country, it belonged to us and he said that he'd do whatever he needed to do to take India back,' said Bibi. She shook her head slowly from side to side. 'Everyone thinks it was Gandhi who drove the white man out of India, but the white man was smarter than that. They hung Bhagat Singh, but there were more and more young men like him, ready to rise up and the white man could see that the tide was turning against them. They knew it would only be a matter of time before their rule was overthrown, so they left, cleaning out India as they went. They took all the diamonds and gold they could, got onto ships and left the whole country in chaos and disarray. I was a young woman by that time, but I've never forgotten. No one would ever be able to forget the things I saw during that time, never.'

Occasionally there's a moment in life when certain things click into place. There were some things that I wasn't sure about before because they had never been explained or openly spoken about. As Bibi talked, I began to see and understand things that hadn't quite made sense before, but I felt a stab of betrayal and sadness because I loved singing the white man's hymns during school assemblies. Now I could understand why my parents were reluctant to interact with white people, why they thought white people were untrustworthy and why some white people thought that they were better than us.

Still trying to get rid of the lump in my throat, I swallowed again. 'Bibi, what happened after the white man left? Did everyone get their things back and live happily again?' In Bollywood films, I'd only seen people live happily ever after.

Bibi's face darkened. 'Oh no...no. How could anyone get their things back? How could they live happily again? Just before they left, the white man divided India. They picked up a pen and just drew a line across the country and out of that line came Pakistan for Muslims and India for Hindus and Sikhs. They refused to let us Sikhs have the Punjab as our own independent country, but the white man was so stupid that they divided Pakistan into two areas split by hundreds of miles with India stuck in the middle. They had Pakistan near Punjab and then across on the other side of India was East Pakistan. Years later that part . . . East Pakistan became a separate country called Bangladesh. You must have heard of Bangladesh?'

I nodded. I had only heard of it because one of my school friends Sadia and her family had come from Bangladesh.

Bibi's voice hardened. 'People started fleeing their homes and villages. If you lived on the wrong side of the line the white man had drawn, you had to move. Muslims left their possessions and homes and walked on foot to whichever side of Pakistan was closest to them at the time. Sikhs and Hindus left with whatever they could carry and rushed to get to the Punjab and India.'

'I remember walking in the searing hot sun, through sand and dust. I must have walked hundreds of miles with my family from Pakistan to the Punjab. We walked through so much violence and killings. Hindus and Muslims and Sikhs all killing each other needlessly. Many people blamed the Muslims for the violence, but the Sikhs and Hindus were just as bad. I know because I saw it all myself. Young children became separated from their families in the chaos and riots. Sometimes children would just be left behind, abandoned by their parents in their panic to save themselves . . . there were many young children left wandering helplessly around without their parents. I saw many babies left on the roadside. Some pregnant women who gave birth during the walk from one country to the other, would have to just dump their newborn baby on the side of the road because there was nothing else to do. Everyone just walked past any abandoned children because they were so desperate themselves. There was no food or water, most people had left their homes in such a hurry with just the clothes on their backs and whatever they could carry in their hands. How could they take on a stranger's child and further burden themselves when they were barely surviving themselves? But it was terrible, it was so terrible.'

'Along the way with hundreds of other villagers, we became trapped by Muslims in a fortress of some sort. I don't remember who built this fortress or exactly where it was. All I can remember is that these Muslims were determined to kill us; I thought I was going to die for sure. There was no police or army to help us and we remained trapped there for three days with nothing to eat and hardly any water. We were finally rescued when more Sikhs turned up and they scared away the Muslims. Then we joined the main trail of hundreds of thousands of people walking to the Punjab. There were so many people! So many people desolate and distressed. I have never seen anything like it before or since! An elderly couple and their teenage granddaughter joined our trail. They told us they'd desperately been fighting off a group of Muslim men who had been trying to carry off their granddaughter. Just as it seemed as if their granddaughter would be snatched away, a Muslim woman had come around the corner and she had screamed and chased the men away. Then this Muslim woman-' Bibi paused to draw breath. 'This woman, who only God could have sent, she escorted this girl and her grandparents to where we were walking and they joined us. That Muslim woman saved that young girl's life.'

'But Bibi . . . why would those Muslim men want to carry off that girl?'

Bibi gave a heavy sigh and I could tell that she was tired.

'Because that's what they used to do in the old days. They'd kidnap girls to sell into brothels or they would marry them and force them to convert to Islam. They weren't interested in taking married women, only unmarried Sikh and Hindu girls. That's why parents married off their daughters while they were still very young because it wasn't safe for girls to remain unmarried. If a girl managed to escape from her Muslim abductors and return to her own family, her family would usually disown her because she's been away from them for several days and nights and so she probably wasn't a virgin anymore. I know lots of stories where a girl's family have rejected their own daughter and they won't have anything more to do with her after she'd been taken by Muslims, even after she escapes and returns home. So lots of girls chose to remain with and marry their Muslim captors and become Muslims. There was a girl who lived next door to us. She was the same age as me, about eleven years old. She was so sweet, good and hard-working, but she was-' Bibi stopped.

Her shoulders slumped, her glazed and downcast eyes stared vacantly at the floor. Bibi was sitting in Walsall, but her thoughts were firmly planted in India.

There was so much more that I craved to know, however not wanting to distress Bibi any further, I quietly left her side. But I wondered whether Bibi really understood that she was now living smack bang in the middle of the white man's country.

'You sound angry Jas and with good reason. The British Empire and its impact isn't openly discussed, is it? And I get the sense that you lived in two worlds, neither of which seems comfortable to you. It sounds as if you were split.'

'Once I knew what white people had done in India, I could understand the undercurrent of resentment that lay in all of the Sikh Punjabis I knew. I could understand why that resentment hadn't faded and why racism went both ways. I'm sure some people will say that the British made India a better place to live and the poor would have been ruled over by the Maharajas anyway. But that's like saying the poor would've been trampled on anyway so it didn't matter who crushed and enslaved them! Or some idiot will mention how the British built extensive railways in India. The railways were built by the blood, sweat and tears of Indians slaving under the orders of the British to make it easier for the British to transport everything they were taking from India.'

'For a while, I couldn't see past the past, if that makes sense? I thought the Indian culture had misgivings, but I was so disillusioned to find out that the English had a shameful past too. I struggled with it because suddenly I felt like no one in the whole world was ever really right and moral and upstanding. Where does one run to for comfort and who does one choose when all sides do wrong? And why is it always...always the innocent who suffer!'

Thirty-Six

Blue Denim Mountains

'Jas come on, up you get.' Bibi nudged me awake.

Reluctantly, I opened my eyes and still full of sleep, I stumbled out of the warm bed. It was 6.30am on a Saturday morning and Bibi and I had to be at work by 8am.

Once Bibi had settled in, my mother had got her a job working in the same factory where my masi had worked. Within a few months of Bibi's arrival, masi had received her British citizenship, remarried and finally left our home, moving to Leicester with her second husband.

Bibi had settled into the work and managed to get me a Saturday job at the same factory. Dimple had been offered the job first, but on account of how she wasn't speaking to Bibi, she'd turned it down.

Bibi had only been living with us for a few months, when an argument between me and Dimple had broken out. The argument had been raging on for over an hour, upstairs and downstairs, in and out of the house. A prolific tea drinker, I made myself a cup of tea in between all the shouting, screaming and chasing. Filling my cup to the brim, as I made my way through the kitchen, Dimple had shoved me, making some of my tea spill, before she ran to the back door. Standing just outside the door, she smirked as she goaded me.

Fearing in my rage that I would throw my scalding hot tea over Dimple, Bibi had quickly stepped forward and locked the back door, leaving Dimple outside the house.

'I wouldn't waste my tea on her ugly face!' I'd screeched, but Bibi had refused to unlock the door and Dimple had remained outside until my parents returned from running their errands.

Believing that Bibi had taken my side, Dimple refused to speak to her. Bibi, having experienced much worse treatment during her life, didn't particularly care. From then on, if she or Dimple had anything to say to each other, my younger sisters and I would be used to relay the message. Though none of my younger sisters nor I would ever have gotten away with being so disrespectful to one of our elders, my parents said nothing to Dimple and allowed the situation between her and Bibi to continue for over a year.

As I got older, arguments between me and Dimple grew frequent. One particularly vicious argument had been raging for almost two hours and in the absence of both my parents, it escalated. I had been trying to do my homework, but Dimple wouldn't stop pushing and shoving me. I didn't even know why she wouldn't leave me alone. Maths was not my favourite subject, so I was already in a foul mood and eventually I had enough. I threw my compass at her head. It missed her by an inch and lodged itself like a dart in the wooden frame of the living room door. Dimple pulled it out, opened the front door and threw my compass into the road. I never got it back, I have no idea where that compass disappeared to!

'Come on Jas, hurry up,' chuckled Bibi. 'Your mum woke up early and made us some parathas. Don't worry, this time . . . I've checked and she's packed the dal and mango chutney this time. You remember last week when she forgot to pack the dal and we had to eat dry roti with just tea? I told her off so she won't forget again. We can't be eating dry roti now, can we?'

'Yes Bibi,' I said as I buttoned up my coat against the early morning chill. It would take us just under an hour to walk to the factory which was situated on the other side of Walsall. Occasionally we'd get lucky and my dad would be around to give us a lift, but that only happened on rare occasions.

The front door of the factory was situated right on the pavement. When we knocked on it, it would open a crack, enough to let us squeeze through before it would be quickly locked behind us.

The factory only produced denim jeans. Bibi worked upstairs in a large room with the rest of the thirty-odd Indian women while I worked downstairs by myself.

When I had first started working at the factory, the owner had pulled me to one side. He told me that I was never to answer the front door if the bell rang, even though I only worked a few feet away from it. Nor was I ever to tell anyone that I worked at the factory.

I nodded at him dumbly, I knew I was underage.

Upstairs the women sat behind rows and rows of sewing machines with their heads bent studiously low. Bibi, who didn't know how to operate a sewing machine, had the job of turning the jeans the right way round for the women and she'd collect and move the piles of jeans around to the right sewing stations ready for the women to put together.

Downstairs the room I worked in was huge. On the floor, strewn all around the room, several piles of jeans were stacked high like blue denim mountains, all in different stages of production. The floor looked like it had never been cleaned, covered with trillions of tiny pieces of broken threads and discarded unusable material. It would have been a job and a half just to clear the floor from all the piles of denim and heavy spun cloth on giant spindles. The whole room was filled with a blue hazy dust which floated up and hung in the air as jeans were flung into piles.

Using small special scissors that made my fingers ache, my job was sniping off any loose threads left over from the sewing stages of production. Wherever I saw loose threads hanging off - on the belt loop, the hems of the jeans, on the back and front pockets or anywhere else, I'd carefully snip them off.

Once we stepped inside the factory, I wouldn't see Bibi again until we had a ten minute tea break in the middle of the morning. We had another ten minute break in the afternoon and we were allowed half an hour for lunch. I'd go upstairs and sit down wherever I could find space on the floor with Bibi and we'd eat together and drink hot tea from our flask.

The women workers would glance over at me and exclaim that I was too skinny, I was too quiet, I was too dark, I didn't eat enough, I wasn't that pretty and that I was too subdued. I'd try and keep out of their way, but once all the sewing machines had been turned off and the radio, which was permanently tuned to an Indian radio station was switched off, it was quiet enough for the women's loud voices to carry from one end of the room to the other. No conversation was private and the women seemed to believe that they were free to interject and interfere with any conversation they happened to eavesdrop on. They would frequently complain to Bibi that I didn't seem to want to engage in any conversations with them.

Bibi would smile and nod politely while I tried to eat as quickly as I could, relieved that I worked mainly in isolation downstairs. I liked the peace and quiet of my room and I was mostly left on my own, save for the odd occasion when Guddi, the teenage daughter of the owner would come downstairs and use the only sewing machine tucked in one corner of the room.

If Guddi's father went out on deliveries and she happened to be using the sewing machine in my room, she would bring down the radio from upstairs, plug it in and turn up the volume. She'd dance and sew at the same time. Moving her shoulders up and down and wiggling her hips on her chair, she'd make me laugh as we giggled and joked together. While upstairs the women were still bent low over their machines, we would all relax. But as soon as Guddi's father returned, a sober silence would strike both downstairs and upstairs and only the sound of the radio and the loud whirring of the sewing machines would be heard.

I felt sorry for Guddi and her mother, who also sat and toiled upstairs at one of the sewing machines. Come 5pm I could leave, but they were both stuck. The owner never seemed happy, his mouth permanently in a downward grump. Guddi was definitely not cut from the same cloth as her father and the time I spent laughing with her - along with the 50p I earned every Saturday - made my first job just about bearable.

'Unfortunately it's a practice that continues to this day in lots of countries Jas, doesn't it? Where children work in factories and financially help to support their families.'

'It does unfortunately. I didn't have to support anyone though. My parents never asked me or my sisters to hand over our wages, whatever they were. My dad opened bank accounts for us as soon as we got jobs and we were encouraged to save our money. Though if we wanted to spend it, my parents never said anything either. I eventually got another job with my sister Sarb working at a supermarket stacking shelves so I left the jean factory.'

'It sounds like your parents instilled a good work ethic in you,' said my therapist.

'Yeah, they did. We worked in the home and at our jobs and we also had to do our homework in the midst of all that big rabble of people who were living in our house. After I left, Bibi carried on working at the factory and the owner

tried to persuade her to make me come back, but I never returned. I missed Guddi though. Whenever I think about her, it makes me sad. Her smile would be determined by the mood her father was in when he was around. It must be very tiring . . . to spend your life enduring someone else's moods. Your day-to-day life and how good or bad it will be, is determined by someone else. It's a ridiculous way to spend your life.'

'Did you ever wonder what made him grumpy Jas? I mean if he's running a business, there's bound to be pressure to make it a success.'

'Even at the time, I did wonder why he was always so grumpy. I mean the factory was always busy churning out jeans, the work for him as the owner must have been never-ending cos you know there's always accounts and the admin side of a business to take care of, but everyone has those pressures in a business. I felt that the only way he could push the women, including his wife and daughter to work even harder for him was by constantly being in a bad mood. His way, I think, was to be scary enough for the workers not to want to push him or displease him because they feared his foul mood getting worse.'

'It's a manipulative way of controlling people and situations. Sometimes it's the only way that a person knows how to engage with other people though,' said my therapist.

'What . . . by making them scared of your moods? I've seen it in other people too. They throw out this thing that says "I'm already in a bad mood so don't push my buttons any further!" And then they get whatever they wanted, exactly in the way that they wanted it without any resistance because everyone is scared of them and nobody wants to set them off!'

Thirty-Seven

An Indian Crush

'Oh my God! Sorry!' Losing my balance, I crashed into a girl, flinging her across the aisle. 'So sorry!'

My first time on a train, I gritted my teeth as I bounced around with the rocking and swaying of the carriage. I stumbled along using the headrests of the seats to keep myself upright and unsteadily I made my way down the narrow aisle and half-fell, half-slid into the seat across from Sarb.

It was the first time that my parents had allowed us to go on a trip with school outside of normal school hours. We were never allowed to go on overnight trips or trips abroad, but for some reason, perhaps because there were two of us going and it was only a daytime outing to go rambling, my parents had agreed to this trip.

With our sandwiches packed, we headed deep into the green countryside. Heavy rain was already pouring down, but I didn't mind. I loved the rain and I was happy just to have been allowed out of the house on a weekend.

I glanced up as Mr Abbott slowly made his way down the aisle. Bobbing his head, he meticulously counted the children in his charge. 'Ok listen up folks! We're going to be arriving at our station shortly, so please gather up all of your belongings. We don't want anything left behind on the train! And please remember to stay together once you're on the platform. Don't go wandering off anywhere...I don't want to have to call in a search party for you!'

As Mr Abbott walked past my seat - that was when I saw him. Sitting a few seats further down the carriage, he was laughing and chatting with his friends. His smile was wide and his dark hair flopped across one of his big brown eyes. He looked so happy and carefree, not like some grumpy moody boy trying to be all dark and mysterious and in an instant I was smitten.

I'd always avoided any contact with boys and I never imagined that I'd have a crush on one, but suddenly I did. Out of nowhere, I finally understood what all the fuss was about. His name was Sunil and he was in the year below me at school. With over a thousand children attending Alumwell and with my nose usually buried deep in a book, if it hadn't been for the rambling trip, I may never have come across him.

I returned to school on Monday and in the hope that he would return my infatuated feelings, I tried to get Sunil to notice me, but I never managed to pluck up the courage to speak to him. Instead I'd take slow detours past his classroom or I would wait for him to walk past me and my friends in the corridor before we'd change direction and follow him back along the corridor, trying and failing to be inconspicuous. I even wrote him a love letter and waited anxiously as a giggling Roshna and Maria delivered it to him. Though I waited with bated breath, I never got any response from him and not knowing what to say to him, I never even tried to speak to him myself. My crush on Sunil lasted almost a year and then just as suddenly as it had ignited, it burnt out. I had simply got bored.

Every other year after Sunil, I'd have a crush on a boy, but none of the boys I fancied ever returned my feelings, so eventually my crush on them would fizzle out and disappear into nothingness. I didn't mind too much. Too shy to approach or speak to any of the boys that I liked, I preferred to admire from afar. Not being allowed to talk to any boys outside of my family meant that I had no real idea how to interact with the boys at school.

One of the boys I fancied had once unexpectedly walked up to me in a crowded corridor and with a big smirk across his face, he said, 'my dog's backside looks better than your face!' He walked off as everyone around me fell about laughing. I didn't understand, all I'd ever done to him was to like him!

Though I felt awful for a long time about his comment, he did me a huge favour. Not only did I immediately stop liking him, but he made me realise that I'd had a lucky escape from him. I wouldn't have wanted to have anything to do with a person like that, let alone be his girlfriend.

Another time, when a boy was told that I liked him, he turned and began to walk towards me to see who I was. But as soon as I realised that he was walking towards me, I panicked and ran like the wind in the opposite direction just to get away from him!

'So how would that have worked if Sunil had returned your feelings and liked you back Jas?'

'That's a scary thought! I never actually thought that far ahead. Maybe deep down I was ok that he didn't return my feelings because then I didn't have to do anything to upset my parents - that kinda sums up an Indian crush.'

'It probably felt like a safe crush because nothing was going to happen,' said my therapist.

'Yeah I had all the feelings, but it was also a secret crush. Secret from my family I mean, not secret from Sunil. He knew because I'd sent him a love letter and I'd follow him around. I couldn't tell anyone apart from my friends because me and my sisters weren't even allowed to talk to boys, let alone have a crush on one.'

'How did that feel though? Because all of your life your parents have stopped you from interacting with boys and then suddenly you have these feelings for a boy and even to have those feelings is forbidden.'

'Well . . . parents can somewhat control their children's actions, but never their children's feelings. When I had that crush on Sunil, with that because of what my parents had always taught me, came feelings of guilt for having a crush. So with the great, weird and wonderful feelings of a crush, hand-in-hand came the awful feeling that I was betraying my parents.'

'It sounds as if your parents were very effective in their conditioning of you. For you to feel guilty about having a crush, a crush is not something that is usually under the control of a person. And it's a very normal and natural thing, isn't it? To feel attracted to someone?'

I nodded. 'My parents were brilliant at the emotional guilt trip to stop us from openly and fully experiencing and accepting normal emotions and feelings, they would say anything to keep us toeing the line.'

Thirty-Eight

Simple For The White Girls

'Donna, wait up!'

At the end of the school day, our teacher had let my class out a few minutes early and I was walking out of school with my friend Donna.

We turned around at the same time to see who was calling her. It was one of the Sikh boys in our year. He quickened his pace to catch up to us.

As Donna and the boy chatted, all three of us continued walking up the school path heading towards the road, but as we approached the pavement in front of the school, I was beginning to feel worried. The boy wasn't going away and we were almost outside of school where anyone could see that I was walking with a boy. Even though she was walking between me and the boy, no one would notice Donna in the middle.

Then as I stepped up onto the pavement in full view of the road, my worst nightmare was realised. My dad's car was parked outside the school with both of my parents sitting in it. I couldn't believe it! Never before (or since) had both of my parents picked me up from school. I felt my stomach drop and I silently groaned. The only time I had ever walked alongside a boy and both of my parents were there to witness it!

The fact that the boy had ignored me and had only talked to Donna would not matter to my parents. I knew I was going to be in trouble, but I wasn't sure how much or what kind.

Mumbling that I'd see her later, I hurried away from Donna and the boy.

'See you tomorrow Jas,' called Donna, oblivious to my panic.

Head down, I opened the back passenger door and slid into the back seat of my dad's car.

'Hello,' I said, pushing myself into the backrest trying to keep out of my mother's reach. I prepared myself to get shouted at and maybe even whacked.

Sitting in the front passenger seat, my mother turned around to face me. 'Jas, do you know that when we first saw you walking with that boy, I told your dad that we were mistaken. I told him that that couldn't be our daughter walking with a boy! Not my daughter . . . that's what I said to your dad. When we've told you a thousand times before, you'd never let us down like that, would you? That can't be our Jas! That's what I told your dad. But when you came closer and I saw that it was really you . . . well . . . I couldn't believe my eyes! We never dreamt that our daughter could do something like that!'

Not saying a word, my dad sat staring straight ahead.

'I don't know that boy. He's that white girl's friend,' I mumbled.

I couldn't understand why I was feeling guilty, as if I really had done something wrong. Maybe I should have shouted at the boy to go away, told him to walk on the other side of the path. Maybe I should have told Donna to ignore him.

'I never even spoke to him,' I added.

'You see! Now do you understand, why you have to be so careful who you walk with, don't you? Now if anyone else had seen you, they'd have thought that that boy was your friend, wouldn't they? Because that boy was with you, they'd have thought that you knew each other, wouldn't they?' Turning back around, my mother faced the front.

Relieved that I hadn't got a whack, I didn't say anything as I stared out of the car window. But my mind was racing. Everything seemed to be so simple for the white girls. Donna was allowed to walk with whoever she wanted and for the first time in my life, I resented being an Indian.

'Sounds very passive-aggressive Jas.'

'What do you mean . . . who was passive-aggressive?'

'Your mother. Trying to make you feel ashamed and guilty.'

'Of course! I don't know why I didn't see it before. That incident always stuck in my head because I expected to get shouted at, but my mother was sickly sweet. She made me feel as though I'd hurt her and my dad even though I hadn't even done anything. I had already done what my parents wanted me to do by ignoring and not speaking to boys as best as I could during my time at school, yet they still made me feel bad. Even though it must have been obvious, even to them that I had no say over who decided to talk or walk with any of my friends. I had no control over what the other kids did at school.'

Thirty-Nine

The Book About Birds

'Oi! Ethiopian!'

'Look at her!'

'Here comes the Ethiopian!'

'Oi skinny!'

The name-calling was followed by hyena-like laughter that rang out across the playground. Head down, I tried to hurry past the group of girls. I dreaded coming across them at break-time because as soon as they'd spot me, they would single me out.

These girls were supposed to be the 'brainy' ones in my year, having been selected to be in all of the top sets for all of the academic subjects. They had a ringleader, a Sikh girl called Ishprat who always instigated and led the name-calling. In the entire time that we'd been at secondary school together, I'd never spoken a word to her, but she would still cajole the girls she hung around with to call me names. I considered some of those girls as friends when Ishprat wasn't around. That was perhaps the most hurtful and confusing part of the bullying - how they would completely transform whenever Ishprat was present.

The name-calling had been going on for a while and I could see no end in sight. I'd always been thin and had never considered my weight to be an issue, but after Band Aid and the plight of starving people in Africa had been broadcast to the world, Ishprat and her friends had latched onto it. Thousands of people were dying from starvation and everyone around the world had seen the heart-breaking images of dying children, yet Ishprat and her friends were using that tragedy to bully me.

'Oi! Don't your parents feed you?'

'Stick! You look like an Ethiopian!'

'Skinny!'

'Go back to Africa, your parents are probably looking for you!'

Trying to ignore the taunts, I was relieved when the bell rang, signalling the end of break-time. I headed to my English class, but as soon as I had taken my seat, I heard Mr Roy, my English teacher call my name.

'Jasvir?'

I looked up. 'Yes sir?' My teachers only ever called me by my full name if I was in trouble. But I couldn't possibly have done anything wrong - I'd only just sat down!

Mr Roy walked across to my desk. 'You've been placed in the wrong set for English. You're to go and join Miss Price's class right away. Do you know where that is?'

I shook my head as Mr Roy explained that Miss Price's classroom was on the first floor, the first room on the right. 'Now go quickly before she starts the lesson. And don't look so worried, she's expecting you.'

'Yes sir.' I grabbed my bag and left as my curious classmates looked on.

Miss Price was the only black female teacher at Alumwell and she had a reputation for not tolerating any nonsense. As I hurried up the stairs, with a sigh of relief, I saw that she was still standing outside her classroom door, escorting her students in.

I came to a stop outside her door. 'Miss . . . Mr Roy sent me up. He said that I was in the wrong set.'

Miss Price turned and looked at me for a moment before she gave me a wide smile. 'You must be Jasvir?'

'Yes miss.'

She indicated with her head. 'Well, in you go then.'

I hesitated.

Miss Price chuckled. 'It's alright, Mr Roy showed me some of your English work. He wanted you to be moved up and after reading some of your work, I thought it was a good idea to get you into my class right away. Is that ok?'

'Yes miss,' I said and feeling a sudden rush of comfort at her words, I walked into my new classroom.

Everyone else had already settled in a few weeks earlier and all the seats were taken, apart from one. The last empty seat was at the very front of the class by Miss Price's desk.

I slid into the chair, but as I did so, I silently groaned. Ishprat and her friends were seated right behind me. They stared at me, but with Miss Price standing right in front of my desk, they didn't say anything.

'Here, you'll need this.' Miss Price handed me a book. 'We're already up to chapter three so you'll have to catch up in your own time.' Miss Price turned to the rest of the class. 'Now today we're going to work on grammar.'

I gave the book cover a quick glance, *To Kill A Mockingbird*. Frowning I set it to one side. I couldn't understand why reading about birds would help improve my English skills.

Later that day, at home after I'd finished my chores, I found a quiet corner and I opened up the book about birds. Turning to the first chapter, I began to read.

The next morning, as I waited outside Miss Price's classroom with the rest of my class, Ishprat and her friends decided to make the most of the opportunity. They had the perfect audience: a bored crowd of children who would be happy to be entertained at my expense.

'Oi! Ethiopian! What stupid teacher decided to put you in our set?'

'Ya should've been moved down a set, not up!'

As the corridor filled with nervous laughter from some of the class, I bit my tongue and remained silent.

Ishprat sneered. 'Miss Price told ya to catch us up, have you even read chapter one? Can you even read?' Laughing she turned to her friends. 'I bet she can't even read English!'

'Actually I've nearly finished it!' It was the first time in all the months of bullying that I'd answered her back. Expecting Ishprat to jump down my throat, I was surprised when a deafening silence filled the corridor.

'Have you?'

Quickly I spun around.

Miss Price had come up behind me.

'Did I hear you correctly Jasvir? Did you say that you've nearly finished the book?'

Trying to ignore the curious and unbelieving stares I was getting from the rest of the class, I nodded. 'Yes Miss. I just have the last three chapters left. It got really late and my mum told me to switch off the light and go to sleep, but I'll try and finish it tonight miss.'

Miss Price nodded as she turned the key and unlocked the classroom door. 'And what did you think of it?'

'The book miss? I loved it miss. But I just can't believe that people can do that to other people. They're so wrong and everyone knows that they're wrong, but they still carry on being wrong. It's not fair miss, it's not fair.' Certain that I wasn't making any sense, I stumbled to a stop. My words sounded stupid and not eloquent or sophisticated as I'd intended.

Miss Price turned to the rest of the class. 'Have any of you finished chapter four like I asked you to yesterday?'

One girl hesitantly raised her hand. 'I have miss.'

Miss Price raised her eyebrows and then she picked out Ishprat and her friends from the crowd and fixed her eyes on them. 'And you girls, did any of you finish the chapter I set you yesterday?'

'Not yet miss.'

'I couldn't miss.'

'Nearly.'

'Sorry miss, I forgot.'

Their embarrassed mumbles were barely audible and Ishprat didn't make any attempt to answer Miss Price.

Her jaw set Miss Price pushed open her classroom door. 'Right! In you all go. Jasvir you go in first please.'

I led the class in and took the same seat that I'd taken the day before as Miss Price walked in and stood behind her desk, watching as the rest of her class silently took their seats.

I was rummaging in my bag for my pencil case, when I heard Miss Price call my name.

'Jasvir?'

I looked up. 'Yes miss?'

Miss Price spoke slowly and loudly. 'Jasvir, is that what you want me to call you?'

My eyes widened as I began to stammer. 'Y-yes, yes miss . . . that's my r-real name. Sorry miss, I meant my full name . . . that's my full name.' I hesitated for a split second, before deciding to take the plunge. 'But I like to be called Jas, miss . . . Jas is short for Jasvir.'

Miss Price smiled wider than I'd ever see her smile again. 'Ok, I'll call you Jas from now on then.' And then she turned her attention to the rest of the class and began the lesson in earnest.

Shell-shocked, knowing that something had just happened, but not knowing what, I managed to mumble. 'Thank you miss.'

The book about birds made two things happen for me. I became Miss Price's favourite student and despite starting behind everyone else, within a matter of weeks I excelled and achieved a steady stream of A's as the rest of the class trailed behind with their B's, C's and occasional D's. And the sound of Ishprat and her taunts stopped - as if someone had abruptly switched off a very loud and noisy radio, Miss Price had silenced my bullies.

'At the time I racked my brain to think of something that I'd done to Ishprat to make her bully me.'

'What made you think that you'd done anything Jas?'

'I dunno, I just thought that if you bullied someone, there had to be a reason, but I couldn't find any. I realize now that there's no reason sometimes, a bully is just a bully because that's just the kind of person that they are.'

'Maybe she bullied the other girls in her gang too, maybe that's why they followed her like sheep,' said my therapist.

'It never crossed my mind that she could've been bullying the girls in her gang. She never said anything to me if she was on her own, if she wasn't surrounded by her gang of friends she'd walk past me quietly.'

'Maybe she had to show them how tough she was by calling you names when they were there to witness it. That might intimidate them and show them that it could happen to them too if they got onto her wrong side. What does that tell you about her?'

I grinned. 'I dunno. Maybe because she was heavy-boned and on the plump side, she was an insecure idiot so she took it out on me who was slim and slender. But bullies come in all shapes and sizes, I should never forget that.'

Forty

Indifference

'What's happened Bibi?' I stood at the foot of the stairs and stuck my head into the living room. It was full of relatives and neighbours, but it was far too early in the morning for visitors and despite the number of people in the living room, an eerie quiet filled the room.

'Your grandfather has died,' said Bibi.

In the early hours of that morning, my grandfather had woken up complaining that he felt ill. My dad had telephoned for an ambulance and it had arrived within a few minutes. The paramedics took my grandfather away on a stretcher, but he'd had a massive heart attack in the ambulance before it managed to reach the hospital.

'It was his time,' murmured an aunt.

'It must have been,' said another. 'The hospital is right behind the house, but he couldn't even hold on for five more minutes.'

As I tried to digest the news that at the age of sixty-five, my grandfather was dead, I couldn't quite believe it. I knew I should feel something, but I didn't. I thought about the only time that I'd had any acknowledgement from my grandfather that I existed.

A few weeks earlier, my grandfather had been lying on the settee and for the first time in my life, on a complete whim I'd asked him for something - a pillow that he was using to rest his head on, even though I didn't really want or need the pillow.

My mother had immediately scolded me and told my grandfather not to give me the pillow, but he'd ignored her. Quietly taking the pillow out from under his head, he had handed it to me. I'd been so shocked at his kindness that I hadn't even managed to thank him.

As news of my grandfather's death spread, more relatives came in through the front door. Suddenly I felt something for my grandfather that made me feel uncomfortable - pity. I was feeling pity for my dead grandfather, but I couldn't understand why.

Suddenly the living room door swung open and my aunt Harjit bustled in from the kitchen with a plate laden with food. 'If no one else is hungry, I'm still going to eat! I'm feeling hungry!' She found a gap on the settee and settled herself in. Glancing around the silent room, she spotted me in the midst of all the subdued relatives.

'Jas, go and fetch my children from upstairs. Tell them to come downstairs, brush their teeth and get their breakfast. If you want some tea, I've made loads. I know people will be coming over today and they'll want to drink tea, won't they? Now don't just stand there staring at my face! People die every day! The rest of us still have to eat though, don't we? Now hurry up and get my children so they can have breakfast before the house gets packed with more visitors.'

As the crowded room shifted uncomfortably in shock at my aunt's indifference, I turned and went back upstairs to fetch my young cousins.

The night before the funeral, my parents told me and my sisters that we weren't allowed to go to the crematorium. In the morning, before he was taken to be cremated, my grandfather's body was brought back to the house. Laid out in his open coffin, everyone filed past saying their final goodbyes.

Even my uncle Manjeet was there. He'd been given special day release for the funeral, though for the entire time, he remained handcuffed to one of the two policemen who accompanied him.

I peered at the first dead body I'd ever seen. My grandfather looked as if he was sleeping. I half expected him to wake, sit up and bang his fist onto the coffee table, making demands and threats, but he didn't move. And just like my grandmother Mama, once his coffin was nailed shut and carried out by the men in my family, making his way through the front door for the very last time, my grandfather was also almost entirely forgotten.

'You sound really hurt Jas.'

'Do I? I guess I am hurt underneath all the anger. I'll never know what it's like to have a grandfather. I mean, a proper grandfather, loving and worldly and kind like a grandfather should be. I never met my mother's father, he died in India when I was still young. And I have no loving memories of my dad's father. What a waste though. When he could've been surrounded by hugs and affection from his granddaughters, he choose to behave like an asshole and none of us wanted to be near him.'

'Maybe your grandfather wasn't the kind of man who knew how to show affection,' said my therapist. 'I think a lot of men from your grandfather's generation were taught never to show their caring or vulnerable side. They themselves had probably never experienced or received affection from their own parents, who never received it from theirs and so it continues through families and makes it hard for them to show a softer and gentler side because sometimes they just don't know how to. Your grandfather didn't have any difficulty in expressing his anger, did he? Maybe growing up, he'd seen and experienced anger from

his own parents so that's all he knew. I also think anger is sometimes an easier emotion to express than hurt or affection.'

I shrugged. 'I think it runs in my grandfather's family to behave badly because my grandfather's brother was all about hugs and affection, but the wrong kind.'

Forty-One

Drowned Out My Voice

'How many times has he done it?' I asked Dimple.

'He does it every time he's come to visit since grandfather died. He comes out of the bathroom and then he loiters around until there's no one else here. He waits until I've poured the tea into the cups and I'm holding the tea tray and then he starts stroking my back and trying to touch me on my front,' she said.

After my grandfather's death, his brother Balwant and Balwant's wife had started to visit us frequently. At first, I believed that he was concerned for us because we were family, after all my dad was his nephew. But after one of Balwant's visits, Dimple had pulled me to one side and told me that he'd been touching her. Pretending that he needed to use the toilet, it would give him an excuse to come into the kitchen where Dimple would be making tea for him and his wife. The bathroom was at the back of the house, only accessible through the kitchen and on his way back from the bathroom, he'd start rubbing Dimple's back trying to fondle her.

'Oh . . . so that's why he waits and only does it when your hands are full, so you can't really fight him off properly because you're holding the tea tray.' I was already deep in thought.

As Dimple nodded, I hatched a plan. We agreed that the next time Balwant came to visit, I'd take the tea in and see if he did anything to me. We didn't have long to wait before he returned the following week with his wife.

As on his previous visits, he walked through the kitchen and into the bathroom. Dimple stood at the stove making the tea, but instead of leaving her to it, this time I stayed with her.

Balwant used the bathroom and then hung about the kitchen as Dimple and I exchanged a knowing glance, she poured the tea into three cups. As Dimple took a tray out of one of the kitchen cupboards and carefully placed the hot cups of tea onto it, Balwant began to shuffle his feet. But this time instead of Dimple carrying the tea in, I stepped forward. As I lifted the tray off the kitchen counter and walked towards the living room, Balwant suddenly sprung forward.

On my heels, he came up right behind me and touched my back and tried to fondle my breasts. Still holding the tea tray, I tried to elbow him off. Leaving him behind as I nudged him away, I practically threw myself sideways into the living room where my mother and his wife sat chatting.

As I placed the tray down in front of the two women, my hands were shaking. No one had ever touched me in that kind of way before and I was shocked. I felt dirty and as if I needed to wash myself all over, but I also felt something else - something strong - anger.

Tea delivered, I turned and walked back to the kitchen. As I came into the kitchen, with a smirk across his face and a look of complete innocence, Balwant calmly strode past me and into the living room, joining his wife on the settee.

Dimple had seen him touching me and her face was pale. For several minutes, both of us stood silently in the kitchen trying to get our breaths back, deep in our own thoughts.

Then I turned to my sister. Her face was white, but it got paler still when I whispered. 'How dare he! Just cos he's grandfather's brother and our eldest relative. He thinks everyone respects him! Coming to our house pretending that he's worried about us and he's trying to comfort us after grandfather's death! Who does he think he is? And what does he think we are? Objects just there to be touched whenever he feels like it! I don't think so! I'm gonna tell mum!'

'What? No you can't! We might get into trouble!' squealed Dimple.

I stared at my sister, I was confused. 'Why would *we* get into trouble?'

She didn't answer, instead she stepped in front of me.

'Get out of my way! I'm telling mum about him!' I tried to push Dimple out of the way as I attempted to squeeze through the gap between her and the fridge.

With a nervous laugh, grabbing at my arm, she tried to block my path. 'No! Don't! You can't!'

'Yes I can! Get out of the way!' Furious and doubting whether Dimple had a brain that actually functioned, I managed to shove her aside and I hurried towards the living room. But I came to an abrupt stop just outside it. From the other side of the door, I could hear Balwant along with his wife, saying his goodbyes to my mother.

I quickly glanced behind me to see if Dimple was following me, but she had retreated into the bathroom and locked herself in. I sighed, I was going to have to do this completely on my own. I decided to wait until I heard the front door close, then I pushed open the living room door.

I approached my mother at her sewing machine. Her head was already bent down and I knew that I had to tell her quickly, before she started the machine and it drowned out my voice. 'Mum?'

'What is it?' She didn't look up.

'Balwant's been touching us,' I said.

My mother's head instantly flew up. Her back straight as a ruler, she fixed me with her eyes. 'What did you just say?'

'Balwant's been touching us,' I repeated.

'Us? Who us?'

'Me and Dimple.'

My mother narrowed her eyes. 'What exactly did he do?'

'When he was here with his wife just now and I brought the tea in for you, he came up behind me when I had the tray in my hands and he ran both of his hands down my back and then he tried to grab my chest, up here. I couldn't push him off properly cos I was holding the tea tray, but I got into the living room as fast as I could.'

As I finished speaking, in one swift movement, my mother stood up from her sewing machine and shouted for my older sister. 'Dimple! Dimple! Get in here right now!'

My mother had never acted so quickly or so efficiently. Once she'd spoken with Dimple, she told my dad straight away. My parents agreed that my dad would speak to Balwant and a few days later, my dad did. He went to Balwant's house and quietly had a word with him. Telling him that he knew what he'd been doing to his daughters and that he wasn't allowed to come to our house anymore, but after my dad returned from Balwant's house and before he'd even finished telling my mother what had transpired between him and Balwant, my mother erupted with fury. My parents differed - they hadn't agreed on exactly how and where Balwant would be spoken to.

'Why did you quietly tell him off in a whisper?' My mother screeched. 'Why didn't you confront him in front of everyone? Then everyone would know what he's been up to! That's the only way to stop these kinds of dirty people – to shame them in the open, in front of everyone! You should have spoken to him in front of all our relatives, including his wife!'

My mother narrowed her eyes at my dad. 'Ah! I bet his wife doesn't even know, does she? I bet you never even told him off in front of her, did you? So she doesn't even know the dirty things he's been doing to my daughters, does she?'

'What do you want from me?' asked my dad. 'Why should I shame him in front of everyone? What's that going to achieve? Isn't it enough that I've pulled him to one side and spoken to him! Now he knows that we know what he's been up to!'

My mother drew in a sharp deep breath and in that short silence, we all held ours.

'We know! Yes we know! But no one else knows! God only knows why you're protecting him! Other people, especially his wife should be the first to be told! She comes to our house and parades around thinking that she's better than everyone else and you didn't even let her know what her precious husband's been up to!'

My dad opened his mouth and then without saying a word, he wisely decided to close it again.

Still fuming my mother turned away from him and back to her sewing, but not before she'd muttered loud enough for my dad and everyone else in the living room to hear. 'Apart from your three brothers, the rest of the men in your family are all the same...disgusting and dirty! That's why you don't mind covering up each other's bad deeds!'

'I was thirteen and I didn't have the name for what Balwant was doing, but I did know from the moment that he touched me that it felt wrong and if it feels wrong, then its wrong. I had never been taught about sexual abuse, not at school or at home. Sexual abuse was never mentioned. I

knew all about 'stranger-danger' from school and from watching TV, but the message was only that you might be murdered by some stranger. No one ever tells you about the other types of abuse that you can suffer. And certainly no one had ever warned me that I needed to be careful from people I knew, people who were family. And really, family members are the people that children should be warned about because they're the ones who are allowed to walk freely into our homes. Family members get the easiest access to children.'

'Did your mother's reaction surprise you?'

'At the time I didn't even think about what my mother's reaction would be. Considering that my mother is the kind of person who likes to sweep things under the carpet and is very concerned about keeping up appearances, on this occasion, I have to hand it to her, she didn't care about anything or anyone. All she cared about was keeping me and my sisters away from Balwant's wandering hands. It's funny though...she'd always been vigilant and careful about anyone getting close to me and my sisters when we were playing with our male cousins and uncles, but when the abuse came, it came in the middle of a normal Saturday afternoon, in our kitchen from one of our oldest and most respected family members while we were preparing to serve him tea!'

'Since then, I've learnt that sexual abuse can occur anywhere and from anyone. One of my young cousins Mina was touched up by a priest. God only knows which gurdwara he'd come from because he certainly wasn't one of the local priests. He'd come to her parents' house to conduct some religious ceremony and he'd called my cousin to him when all of the grown-ups were busy elsewhere and he'd tried to touch her between her legs. She'd told her mother, who told everyone else and the priest was immediately thrown out of the house. In that respect, the women of my family weren't completely useless when it came to looking out for their daughters!'

'I know from some of my other clients who have experienced sexual abuse that unfortunately they weren't able to speak out. For a variety of different reasons, people don't feel able to speak out, but you did.'

'I only managed to speak out because my overriding feeling was one of anger. To stop something bad or wrong from continuing to happen, you have to allow yourself to get angry about it and let your anger overtake your fear. Being scared of something doesn't stop it from happening. What I didn't understand was Dimple and why she tried to stop me from telling our mother.'

'Do you think your sister was too scared to tell? Maybe she thought she wouldn't be believed?'

'It never once crossed my mind that I wouldn't be believed, so I don't know what my sister was thinking. My mother never questioned if I was telling the truth, she just knew that I was. I can't fathom why someone wouldn't tell though. I can't even comprehend it, I just don't understand it. It makes no sense to me not to tell if someone is doing something wrong to you, unless you believe that telling won't make any difference. But even then, unless you tell, you won't know for sure if it'll make any difference.'

'Maybe Dimple didn't know how to react or what to do Jas. People deal with uncomfortable subjects in their own different ways and from all that you've told me about your sister, I get the sense that you're very different from each other.'

I nodded. 'That we are! Despite my mother's raging, not all of my dad's relatives were perverts. My dad had this huge, enormous uncle from Bradford who'd come and stay, usually for two or three weeks at a time and he never touched us or behaved inappropriately. He was married, though his wife and children never came to our house with him. He'd come and sit on our settee and eat and talk and sleep. Even Bibi, who loved cooking and entertaining would tire of him by the time he left.'

'I think every family has a relative who they dread turning up at the front door,' said my therapist.

'He was ok, at least he kept his hands to himself! His opinions were another matter entirely. He was free to come to our house and criticise us about things like our clothes, what we watched on TV, what we ate, etc, etc. He had an opinion about everything. I could never understand what he had to gain by being so critical. We didn't live the way he wanted us to live, but why can't people just let others be?'

Forty-Two

Outshone The Lot Of Them

'What's going on? Why's Paula upset?' I asked Maria and Devinder.

Emerging from the entrance to the time tunnel, our friend Paula, red-faced and tearful, had rushed straight past us and through the doors of the maths block.

At the far end of the sports field lay a huge underground tunnel. The tunnel ran underneath the M6 motorway. About a hundred yards long, tall and as wide as two double-decker buses, it was probably used during the construction of the motorway. The tunnel was surrounded by myth and legend, rumours and scary stories abound about time travel and mysterious things happening to people who walked through it. Previous generations of Alumwell had aptly named it the time tunnel.

On the other end of the time tunnel there was a clearing, surrounded by small green slopes and overgrown shrubbery and wild flowers with several metal pipes running across a stream. Once you were on this side of the time tunnel, only a gentle humming of the busy motorway overhead could be heard. Quiet and tranquil, it was an ideal place to go exploring once you'd made it through the time tunnel in one piece!

'You know why Paula's crying?' asked Devinder.

Maria shook her head. 'I dunno, she was fine this morning.'

As we glanced around, one of our other friends Violet also emerged from the entrance of the time tunnel. She too looked weepy and upset.

'What's the matter Violet?' asked Maria.

'Nothin,' muttered Violet as she hurried past with her head down and disappeared through the same doors as Paula, into the maths block.

As Maria, Devinder, and I wondered what might have happened to our friends, we were joined by Roshna and Sadia.

'I told 'em not to go into the time tunnel, but they didn't listen, did they?' said Sadia. 'Both of them have been spending too much time in there. I bet something's happened between 'em!'

For the last few months at dinnertimes, I'd taken to going off school grounds with my friends and walking through the time tunnel emerging out on the other side. But whereas the novelty had slowly began to wear off for the rest of us, Violet and Paula had taken to disappearing into the time tunnel on their own.

Now it seemed that they'd had an argument or a disagreement about something, but no one seemed to know what about. But by the end of the day, rumours started to circulate that as they'd been walking through the time tunnel together, Violet had tried to kiss Paula, but Paula hadn't wanted to be kissed.

The next morning, I had history class with Violet. 'Hey Violet,' I said as I plonked my bag down and took the chair next to her.

'Hi Jas,' she mumbled. She gave me a small smile, but I noticed that her eyes were red and swollen.

By the end of that morning, apart from me and Maria, everybody else was avoiding Violet. While I couldn't understand why Violet would want to kiss Paula, I didn't worry too much about it. To me, she was still Violet, albeit with a new side to her.

Maria and I advised Violet to try to talk to Paula, but though we tried not to make a drama out of what had happened in the time tunnel, Roshna, Sadia and Devinder had an entirely different attitude. Ironically, it was the first and only time that Devinder would ever share the same view as Roshna and Sadia - all three wanted Violet excluded from our friendship circle.

I'd never taken sides against any of my friends before. My group of friends was already beginning to fragment as we'd progressed through our secondary school years, but I struggled to believe that any of my friends had the capacity to turn on each other. While Devinder and Sadia had a hard exterior, Roshna was a sweet and unassuming girl. Yet despite their outer differences and their religions - Devinder was a Sikh and Sadia and Roshna were Muslims - inside all three harbored outdated and prejudiced notions and had handed down their narrow-minded judgement towards a girl they'd been friends with for years.

And worse still was that they expected me and Maria to do the same, but I wasn't going to ignore Violet or treat her differently in any way. It would take several weeks before Roshna, Sadia and Devinder realised that Maria and I weren't going to turn our backs on Violet. Eventually, Paula began to speak to Violet again and an uneasy truce settled in our friendship group.

But during any battle inevitably there will be casualties and not even waiting to sit her exams, Violet left Alumwell.

Violet outshone the lot of them in every area of school life. She was brainy, pretty and sporty, whereas Roshna, Sadia and Devinder couldn't even catch a ball if their lives depended on it, never mind being able to do anything else of talent or significance.

'I don't understand how straight people have managed to get away with mistreating gay people so badly for so many years. Don't straight people have anything better to do than stick their big fat noses into other people's sex lives?'

'Why do you think that they do that Jas?'

'I don't know! Maybe because the world has always got to be picking on somebody, anybody. You only have to look back in history. If it's not gay people, then it's women. If it's not women, it's black people. If it's not black people, then it's Jews. The world cannot rest until someone is being persecuted for something or other!'

'People hold certain beliefs and they fear anyone who is different from themselves and they're not willing for those beliefs to be challenged. You can't grow if your views and beliefs aren't open to be challenged or changed, though it's not a pleasant experience to be challenged,' said my therapist.

'I know . . . I've had my viewpoint challenged and then changed and guess what? It's not the end of the fucking world!'

Forty-Three

This One Is For You, Af

'Jas, this is Af. She wanted to come over and say hello,' said Roshna.

I glanced up from where I was sitting with Maria. I already knew Af by sight. She looked like a lanky giraffe and as if she wasn't tall enough already, she wore heels. Her long, black hair swung loosely around her hips, her clothes always clung tightly to her curves, her cheeks were brushed with pink blush and she wore bright red lipstick smeared across her lips which always seemed to hang open in a wide grin. Even now she was standing next to Roshna with a big smile plastered across her face.

Hi,' I said and I turned back around, not bothering to hear her reply.

Af and her two older sisters were not like any of the other Muslim girls at Alumwell. Openly flirting and throwing coy glances at all the boys, they wore full faces of make-up and could be found constantly preening themselves in front of the mirrors in the girl's toilets before they'd pout and strut down the corridors.

Af was everything that I'd been raised not to be: vain and flirty, she walked with a swagger of her hips and she was always grinning as if she didn't have a care in the world. Somehow she'd become an acquaintance of Roshna's.

The following morning, as I headed out of my English class, I heard someone call my name. Looking up, I saw Af.

'Hi!' She flashed her wide grin at me.

'Oh . . . hi.' Taken aback by her presence outside my classroom, I carried on walking down the corridor. Much to my annoyance, Af fell into step beside me.

Her next words stated as a matter of fact, shocked me. 'You think you're too good for me, don't you?'

Mortified that she could be so frank and flabbergasted that she'd read me so well, I stumbled around for an answer. 'Oh . . . no . . . no . . . I don't . . . I don't.' I expected Af to look hurt or be angry, but instead she tossed her head back and laughed out loud.

She grinned. 'You don't lie very well, do you?'

I fell into an embarrassed silence. I'd assumed Af was stupid because she only cared about how she looked and how many boys she could attract, but somehow she'd managed to read me perfectly. Clearly she wasn't a complete airhead.

As we continued down the corridor, I noticed that every boy who walked past us had stared open-mouthed at her with their eyes wide as saucers. Af was swinging her hips and grinning like the cat who'd got the cream. Part of me felt so uncomfortable with all the attention she was generating that I wanted to get away from her as quickly as I could, but a part of me also wanted to put her in her place. I turned to her. 'Can't you even walk down the corridor without putting on a fucking show?'

To my amazement, Af exploded with laughter. 'Oh my God . . . you're so funny Jas!'

With growing infuriation, I begrudgingly plodded along, wishing that either Af would magically disappear or that I could. She chuckled softly all the way to the doors which led to the playground, but in the throng of other children, I managed to lose her.

A few days later as I chatted with my friends at dinnertime, Af walked across to us. With a big smile, she greeted everyone, but her eyes came to rest on me.

'Hi Jas.'

Not inclined to be cruel, I gave her a short smile. 'Does anyone wanna come to the shops with me?' she asked.

I opened my mouth to tell her I didn't, but to my surprise my friends readily agreed to go with her. Not wanting to be left behind, I trailed after them, but Af waited for me and fell into step beside me. As she chattered away, she didn't seem to notice that I barely spoke a word as we made our way up the road to the local newsagents.

I bought my favourite chocolate Bounty and left the shop with a few of my friends. We stood outside and waited for Maria and Af to come out, but as we stood on the pavement, we noticed that a car full of boys had pulled up and parked a few yards away from the shop. As soon as Maria and Af emerged from the shop, the driver pulled down his car window and leaned out.

'Oi you! Come over here, I wanna talk to you.'

The rest of us bristled, but without any hesitation, Af flicked her long dark hair over one of her shoulders and hips swaying from side to side, she ambled across to the car.

I rolled my eyes and raised my eyebrows at Roshna as she blushed.

'Come on guys, let's go,' said Roshna, sounding flustered as she started to walk back down the road, heading for school.

The rest of my friends followed her, but for some reason, I didn't want to leave without Af. I looked over at her, she was leaning into the car, chatting and flicking her hair.

As I stood undecidedly, the driver stretched his neck out of the car. 'Oi you! Come here, I wanna talk to you as well!'

I saw Af's face fall and for a few seconds she appeared as though she was suddenly lost.

Ever since I'd started at Alumwell Comprehensive, I'd seen cars full of boys cat-calling and whistling to girls, but I had never attracted their attention before.

Now as I made my way to the car, I said a silent prayer that my parents would never find out that I had gone when I was called. I stopped right by the driver's door.

His wide smirking mouth showed off his crooked, decaying brown teeth. 'So what's your name then?' he asked.

Ignoring him and his question, I took Af by her elbow and gave her a light tug away from the car. 'Come on, let's go. You're not staying here.'

For a second, Af looked completely confused.

Then without a word, she turned with me.

As we both walked away, I saw the driver's face fall. 'Oi you! Oi!' He was clearly annoyed that he'd lost the chance to hit on Af.

Up ahead, I saw Roshna and the others standing still, huddled together. I waved at them. 'We're coming Rosh.' They let out a collective sigh of relief and continued walking down the road.

'Did you see all those boys that wanted me Jas? Did you see 'em? Did you see how they were looking at me? See I can have anyone!' Af was talking fast. 'They wanted me, but they can't have me so they went for you instead! I wasn't going to go with that boy, no way! I can get much better than that guy! Guys go crazy over me all the time!'

As Af talked non-stop, walking silently beside her, I had no doubt that Af could get any boy she wanted. But for the first time since I'd met her, Af didn't have a bounce or a swagger in her walk. I realised that I needed to say something, but I didn't know what to say.

I looked down at the Bounty in my hand. I opened the wrapping and turned to her. 'Here, this one is for you Af.'

She looked at the chocolate and hesitated.

I held it towards her. 'It's fine, just take it.'

To my relief, she reached out and took one of the chocolate bars. 'Thanks.'

I smiled. 'So how do you put on your lipstick so that it doesn't smudge all over your teeth?'

Back in her element, Af relaxed and by the time we'd made our way back to school, her bounce had returned and I knew all about the complexities of applying lipstick.

Despite my reservations and all of our differences, Af and I became inseparable after that day.

But a few weeks later, at home my dad summoned me to him. 'Jas, you're friends with that Af girl? You know she's a Muslim, don't you?'

I frowned. How did my dad even know Af's name? I'd never spoken about any of my school friends at home. Clearly I was being spied on. I shouldn't have been surprised. I didn't know any Sikh Punjabi, Hindu or Muslim girls who hadn't been spied on. It was considered normal for our parents to spy on us. A lot of parents openly boasted about watching their daughters when they were outside the home. I knew that some members of my own family sat outside their daughters' schools and watched their daughters' comings and goings. But until now I'd had no idea that my own parents were capable of doing the same.

'Do you know what she is?' asked my dad. 'She's not a good girl, ok? I've seen her myself talking to boys. You're not to be friends with her anymore. Do you understand? There are plenty of other girls that you can be friends with. There must be lots of Sikh girls at your school that you can choose as friends who won't lead you down the wrong path like this Muslim girl!'

I couldn't tell my dad that there were lots of Sikh girls at my school who had walked 'down the wrong path' many times over and I knew that Af didn't sleep around with guys, but even if she did, that was her business. With growing anger, I listened silently to my dad as two thoughts swirled around inside my head. He'd spied on me and he was a hypocrite. But not saying anything, I simply nodded when he asked if I understood everything that he'd just explained to me about Af. Satisfied, my dad left the room, however I had no intention of obeying him.

But my dad wasn't the only one who had a problem with me and Af being friends. At school, Af's older sisters would openly make snide comments to me while they glared at Af. They didn't want her hanging around with a Sikh girl, but Af always shrugged them off. Refusing to listen to them and refusing to let go of our friendship, it never even crossed our minds to stop talking to each other just because other people wanted us to.

'How come you didn't wanna talk to them boys?' Af asked me one day, long enough after the incident with the boys in the car that she was comfortable bringing it up.

Sitting with her on the radiator in one of the corridors, I shifted uncomfortably. Out of all my friends, only Roshna knew about Kabir. I didn't know how to explain to Af that having fun with boys in cars wasn't all that it was cracked up to be and that I'd never even remotely been interested in boys who drove up and down the streets hunting for schoolgirls.

I shrugged. 'I'm not allowed to talk to boys. You know how our parents are. They think that just because you talk to a guy, it means that you're sleeping with him and then no one is going to want to marry you. If my parents ever saw me talking to some guy in a car, I'd get killed on the spot! You know what they're like!'

Af flicked her hair over her shoulder. 'My parents think I'm going to marry my cousin in Pakistan, but I'm not going to marry him! I think it's disgusting to marry your own cousin.'

It was the first time Af had told me that she was engaged to her cousin in Pakistan. As she spoke, I was overcome with a sudden feeling of being suffocated. The corridor I was sitting in, suddenly seemed narrow and gloomy and I felt as if I was being covered by a dark and heavy blanket. Finding myself struggling to draw breath, I felt a lump in my throat. I wanted to tell Af not to go. That she should never get onto a plane bound for Pakistan. That she should never leave the safety of England.

'Jas? What's wrong?' Af had stopped talking about her fiancé and she was staring at me. 'You look like you're about to die! You ok?'

I managed to swallow and the dark blanket around me began to evaporate. The corridor became wide and bright again and the sunshine beamed warmly through the big windows. The noisy hustle and bustle of children as they enjoyed their dinnertime pierced through my lingering feelings of darkness.

I felt unsteady on my feet as I stood up. 'I'm fine.' As I tried to reassure Af, I couldn't explain what had just happened, but I hesitated. Maybe I should try and stop Af, maybe I should tell her what I had just felt. Maybe I should tell her that going to Pakistan was the wrong thing for her to do. I should say something or do something . . . anything.

'Let's go outside Jas, you look like you need some fresh air,' said Af. As she took me carefully by the arm and led me outside, I said nothing.

As Af and I slowly wandered arm-in-arm through the playground, silently I scolded myself - I was being silly. Nothing was going to happen to Af. She was smart and strong enough to take care of herself. If she didn't want to marry her cousin in Pakistan, then she wouldn't marry him. It was very simple really. We lived in England, not in Pakistan or India, so no one could make us do anything that we didn't want to do. I didn't need to feel suffocated by a strange darkness because clearly I was imagining things. By the time the bell rang signaling the end of dinnertime, I'd managed to brush aside the dark feelings I'd had about Af.

A few days later, Af and I were sitting on the same radiator in the same corridor.

'What're you gonna be when you grow up Jas?' Af asked.

I bopped up and down in my excitement. 'I'm going to be a journalist! I'm going to work in Fleet Street and write stories about all the things that are happening in the world.'

Af screwed her nose up. 'What's Fleet Street?'

'It's where all the great journalists work, it's in London. Only the best journalists work in Fleet Street and one day I'm gonna work there too!'

Af giggled. 'When you get to Fleet Street, will you write a story about me?'

As I hooted with laughter, Af protested.

'I'm very beautiful and interesting! You can write about me and then the whole world will know how beautiful I am. Oh come on Jas, will you please write about me?'

Laughing I rolled my eyes at her. 'Ok! If you ever do anything interesting, then I'll write about you ok?'

'You promise?' Af grinned, delighted at the thought that at some time, somewhere in the future, she might be mentioned in a newspaper.

I chuckled. 'Yes . . . I promise! Cross my heart and hope to die!'

A few months later, Af did something very interesting. One day she was there at school and we were laughing and joking together and the next she went to Pakistan and didn't come back.

'I should have said something the very first time I heard about her engagement. Every time I think of Af, I feel as if I can't breathe, that I'm suffocating. I can't explain it. Wherever she is, I wasn't there for her, was I? I did nothing and when I did nothing at the time, then how can I cry and complain now?'

I looked out of the window. 'I think Af realised that her world would shrink, especially if she went to Pakistan and got married to a guy and lived over there. She'd have been surrounded by Muslims all of her life then. She may never really have another chance to have a Sikh friend or a black friend again. I'm sure there are some towns and cities in Pakistan which are diverse where all religions, races and cultures intermingle, but I don't think there are many. Sometimes I think we forget how lucky we really are, to be living in a country like England where everyone mingles and we have a chance to get to know people from different cultures and different religions.'

'Do you think people living here recognize or even understand that Jas? To have that world view and how important it is?'

'Maybe some of them do, but others never will. Even when I was at school, I'd see people clash simply because they came from different religions. I've clashed myself a few times over religion, but not in the way you'd think.'

Forty-Four

Make Sure You Remember This

'Alright Jas,' said Rajan as he sat down next to me.

'Hi,' I smiled at him.

Rajan was a friend of two Sikh girls, both named Mahinder, who were in my art and science classes. I'd bonded with them over our mutual love for Don Johnson and Miami Vice and though I still maintained a distance from all boys, if Rajan ever wandered over to hang out with the two Mahinders, I'd be polite and say hello. Rajan was part of the Sikh gang at school and unfortunately both Mahinders were infatuated with the gang.

I didn't particularly like the Sikh boys in my year, especially those who were part of the gang. While a few of the Sikh boys in my school were nice enough, the majority of them behaved like egoistical twits. Only interested in chasing white girls and bossing around the Sikh girls who were stupid enough to listen to them. Despite not being academic or sporty or having any other tangible talent to speak of, the gang of Sikh boys would parade around the school as if they owned it.

The recitals in the gurdwara had taught me that Sikhs were supposed to be humble, brave, tolerant and caring. The Sikhs who founded Sikhism, the Sikhs who fought the Sikh-Muslim wars and those Sikhs who fought in both world wars on behalf of the allies were all noted for their bravery and sacrifice. But since then, that rightfully-earned and well- deserved reputation has been misused by all kinds of hypocritical and arrogant Sikhs. The only Sikh boys I cared about were those who made music, beat the bhangra dhol and spread the joy of song and dance.

Spotting Roshna and Sadia on the other side of the playground, I got to my feet. 'I'll see you guys later, I'm gonna hang out over there,' I said to both Mahinders. Both Mahinders refused to talk to any of the Muslim girls.

'Where you going Jas? I just got here!' said Rajan.

Casually I bobbed my head. 'Over there to Roshna.'

Scowling Rajan stood up. 'Why you going over there?'

Taken aback, I frowned. I hadn't expected Rajan to even notice or care, let alone question me.

'Why you gonna go over to them for? You know they're Muslims, don't you?' asked Rajan.

I rolled my eyes. Why was *that* always the question that was asked? 'Course I know they're Muslims! But they're still my friends.'

'How can Muslims be your friends Jas? Don't you know what they did to us?!'

'Actually I do know, but it wasn't my friends that done it, was it?' I shrugged and turning, I walked away. Rajan glared at me, but he didn't say anything else or try to stop me.

A few days later as I chatted with both Mahinders, Rajan wandered over. As he flopped himself down next to us, deliberately loud enough for everyone around us to hear, he said, 'you smell Jas!'

As both Mahinders began to titter, I stared at him in shock, dumbfounded.

'I'm serious man. You smell Jas. You stink really badly!' Rajan jeered as both Mahinders giggled along. Not saying anything, I got up and walked away.

It was the beginning of a campaign of bullying and abuse that would last for months. After that day, whenever Rajan would see me, he would start to taunt me about my weight, my clothes, my hair, the way I smelled and the fact that I was bad at maths. But then he began to say things about my parents and how they couldn't really be Sikhs because they'd raised a lover of Muslims.

'You better shut up Rajan!' I finally answered him back after he started abusing my parents. But no sooner had the words left my mouth, than for the first time since the bullying had started, one of the Mahinders stepped in.

Forcefully she led me away. 'Leave him alone Jas. You know this is all your own fault, you're the one who hangs around with Muslims.'

I shrugged her off my arm. 'What?' I'd noted that she had done nothing when Rajan had been picking on me, but the minute that I'd stood up for myself, she'd quickly stepped in to protect him.

'The Sikh boys don't like it when they see a Sikh girl with Muslims. You know you're not supposed to be friends with 'em. You know what they did to us.'

I spun away from her. 'I'm a Sikh so I can only have Sikh friends? Is that what you're trying to tell me? You think I'm gonna let any stupid Sikh guy tell me who I can or can't be friends with! When do they ever ask you who they can be friends with, huh? They hang around with whoever they want...white, yellow, brown and then they think that they're gonna tell me what to do! It's not up to them or you who I hang around with!'

Mahinder scowled. 'You're just being stupid.'

'Well, at least I'm not up anyone's ass like you! You know something, just piss off!' And with that, I decided I would stop hanging around with the Mahinders. That meant I was out of Rajan's grasp...almost.

Unfortunately my science class was joined to Rajan's and he would have to pass through my classroom to get to the science lab for his lesson. Three times a week, I'd take my seat at the start of my science class with trepidation, knowing that there would be no escape because Rajan never failed to make the most of the opportunity.

'Oi look! It's smelly!' Rajan called out one day as soon as he spotted me. Surrounded by his friends, he laughed and the class giggled along with him. I hoped with the smelly insult that he was done and he would move along to his own classroom, but he had an audience who had nothing to do until our science teacher arrived.

'I don't think your parents feed you . . . look how skinny you are! Look at your hairy legs, you look like a monkey!'

The classroom filled with the sound of sniggers as I shifted uncomfortably in my seat. Keeping my eyes on the board at the front of the classroom, I tried to tune everyone out. Silently I prayed that my teacher would show up and my torture would be over.

Suddenly I felt something brush against my hair and I heard Rajan laugh.

I spun around. 'What're you doing?! Don't touch my hair!'

Rajan grinned as his friends tried to hide their smirks.

With a sickening feeling in the pit of my stomach, I watched as Rajan licked the palm of his hand and waved it towards my head. I turned and twisted as I tried to dodge his wet hand. His friends, both Mahinders and the rest of the class gathered into a crowd.

'Stop it! Get away from me Rajan!'

Instead he stepped closer. He laughed as he moved his wet hand towards my head. I swung my body around, so I could get out of my chair and get away from his wet hand, but as I stood up I suddenly felt complete and utter rage.

Rajan was in mid-laugh when I grabbed him by his hair and charged him up against the classroom wall. I bashed his head against the hard brick of the wall and pushed my forearm as hard as I could against his throat. Somehow I'd managed to pin him against the wall. His arms were flailing and flapping around as he tried to hit me back, but I was so furious I didn't feel anything. I kept my arm pressed against his throat as I let go of his hair and punched him again and again in his stomach. One of the Mahinders tried to pull me off him, but my grip and fury were so strong that she couldn't budge me.

'Jas . . . you're choking him!! Let him go . . . for God's sake . . . let him go! He's going to choke!'

Rajan's friends had stood watching and laughing at first, believing that he'd be able to fight me off. How could a girl as slight as I was win in a fight against a boy? But it quickly became apparent that I was beating the crap out of him. When Mahinder wasn't able to help Rajan, two of his friends tried to pull me off him, but even they struggled to release my grip as I managed to grab Rajan's hair again and bash his head against the wall.

From somewhere behind me, one of the Mahinders cried out. 'He's choking Jas! Just let him go!'

I pressed my forearm down hard against Rajan's throat one last time. 'Next time you think of opening your mouth in front of me, make sure you remember this!'

Then I released him and stepping back, I shrugged off his friends. 'Piss off, will you? Don't fucking touch me!'

One of the Mahinders quickly pulled me away and Rajan's friends rushed to gather around him, just as my teacher walked into the classroom.

In the blink of an eye, the crowd of children separated and dispersed, all of them acting as though nothing had happened.

But my science teacher realised that something was amiss. 'What's going on in here? What's just happened?'

Two children from the crowd answered him as quickly as they could.

'Nothin' sir.'

'Dunno sir.'

Frowning my teacher turned to Rajan's friends. 'Boys?'

'Nothin' sir.'

'I dunno . . . nothing.'

Rajan's friends tried not to look in my direction. Behind them, leaning against the wall for support, Rajan tried to straighten himself out. He was bright red, dishevelled and dazed.

My teacher glanced around the room. His eyes passed over me, but then just as quickly they returned to study my face. I was red and breathing hard. But then perhaps believing that I was such a quiet and reserved girl, that whatever had happened in his classroom could not possibly have had anything to do with me, he shrugged his shoulders in quiet resignation at the collective wall of silence and he turned to Rajan and his friends. 'This isn't your classroom, you boys shouldn't even be in here. Move along please.'

As my teacher headed to the front of the classroom, I retook my seat. As Rajan and his friends passed behind my chair, for the first time in months, I sat without cowering. My feelings of anxiety and nervousness at Rajan's presence had gone, completely vanished.

As I opened my science book, one of the Mahinders leaned across to me. 'Man . . . you proper battered him Jas!' she whispered. 'God you're strong!'

'I wasn't strong, I was just furious. My only regret was that I waited so long before I whacked him. I don't think he'd ever have stopped bullying me if I hadn't whacked him like I did, though even I was surprised at the rage that came out of me!'

My therapist gave me a lop-sided grin. 'I don't think Rajan was expecting you to have that kind of rage either!'

'He definitely wasn't! I completely caught him off guard. After that day, he never even looked in my direction again and if we ever passed each other in the corridor, he'd divert his eyes away from me and walk on by without a word. In my school, the rivalry between Sikhs and Muslims made everything so much worse.'

'But why do you think the rivalry was there in the first place?'

'I think because a lot of the Sikh boys in my school were spoilt by their mothers. They had been raised to believe that they were the best, mummy's precious little princes, better than anyone else. They disliked anyone who was different to them and they looked down on Sikh girls, white boys and in particular Muslims. There was the history of religious wars and violence between Sikhs and Muslims in India, so it became this mish-mesh of history mixed with past wrongs mixed with arrogance mixed with ego mixed with self- righteousness. I didn't even know how bad things had become between the two gangs until something happened. Something that was so notorious it became the talk of Alumwell.'

Forty-Five

Quietly Satisfying

'Where is he?' asked Clare.

'I dunno.' Shrugging, I glanced up and down the corridor.

Our geography lesson should have started thirty minutes ago and though our classroom door had been left wide open, there was no sign of our teacher, Mr Frederick. Along with the rest of my class, I milled around, in and out of the classroom. Eventually tired of standing, some of the class started to take their seats.

I sat down at one of the desks at the back of the classroom. I had no idea why Mr Frederick was late, but I didn't mind. Geography was not my strongest subject and Mr Frederick was not my favourite teacher. I thought that my luck was in and the bell was going to ring for the end of school before Mr Frederick could appear, when suddenly he strode into the classroom.

Students who were still milling around quickly scrambled for their seats. I noticed that Mr Frederick looked sweaty and browbeaten as he made his way to the front of the class. He didn't even bat an eyelid as a couple of the boys who'd been standing on top of their desks, quickly ducked their heads, jumped down and slid into their seats.

Giving no explanation as to why he was so late, Mr Frederick launched straight into the lesson. 'Right kids, quiet please, let's get on. Turn to page 56 of your text books.'

However by the next day, most of the school knew why Mr Frederick had been late.

'Really? No way! Why would anyone do that?' I couldn't believe my ears at what Roshna was telling me as we slowly walked down the corridor to the dining hall.

The day before while I'd been waiting and wondering where my geography teacher could be, poor Mr Frederick had been at the front of the school trying to talk a machete out of the hands of a Muslim boy called Azad.

Azad had brought a machete into school so he could cut off the head of a rival Sikh boy. Frantic teachers had called the police as Mr Frederick had tried and eventually managed to talk Azad into handing the weapon over to him before he hurt someone.

I'd never heard of this Azad guy before, but Roshna had.

'He lives just down the road from me. I know his parents. I feel really bad for 'em. They're so nice and quiet. They're not going to want their son to be in a gang, are they?' Roshna shuddered. 'God knows what's going on with these boys and their gangs! I don't know why they all have to act so stupid?!'

I nodded. 'I bet he's a proper psycho. Imagine bringing a machete into school! No wonder Mr Frederick was late for our lesson yesterday. Even when he came in he didn't look right, he kept mopping his brow!'

As Roshna and I joined the rest of our friends in the dinner queue, I put all thoughts of Azad out of my head.

I had no time for the stupidity of the boys in my school or their little band of followers, be they Muslim or Sikh. But as I grabbed a tray and asked the dinner lady for some chips, little did I know then, that if I ever asked him, Azad would follow me anywhere.

'So Azad was the leader of a gang . . . a gangster?'

I shook my head. 'No . . . he wasn't a gangster, though he was in a gang. The Sikh gang had ruled our school for years, because the Muslim gang didn't have a leader. Then Azad came along and all the Sikh boys who used to parade around school bragging about how strong and brave they were, ran screaming from him. I'm not gonna lie - that was quietly satisfying.'

Forty-Six

As Light And As Free

'How many times do I have to call you to get onto the coach Jas? This isn't like you at all!' Standing outside the coach door, Mr Wainwright shot me a quizzical look. 'Are you alright?'

The rest of my class had boarded the coach several minutes earlier and already settled into their seats, when Mr Wainwright having counted all of his students, found that he was one down.

'Sorry sir. I'm ok sir,' I mumbled as I trudged up to the coach.

Mr Wainwright rolled his eyes and sighed. 'Alright, up you go then! Quickly! Now that everyone's finally here, we can head back to school!'

I climbed up the steps of the coach with Mr Wainwright on my heels as the driver started up the engine. I managed to throw myself into an empty seat just as the coach lurched forward and turned out of the gravel car park, swinging heavily onto the main road.

As the coach swayed me back and forth, I craned my neck to catch a glimpse of the place we were leaving, my heart longing to remain there.

'What's up Jas?' Seated across the aisle, my friend Kully leaned over to me. She was one of the girls in my English class, always cheery and uncomplicated, I liked her a lot.

I shrugged. 'Nothin . . . I just feel like I should be over there, that's all.'

Kully frowned. 'Over where Jas? Here? You want my seat? We can swap if you like?'

'Oh no . . . no thanks.' I didn't want Kully's seat. I managed to smile at her, before I turned to gaze vacantly out of the window, barely noticing the countryside flying past.

By the time the coach had turned onto the motorway to continue its journey back to Alumwell, I'd already determined that after I died, I wanted my ashes to be scattered in the orchard that I'd just visited with my class.

When I'd stepped into the orchard, I had felt complete and utter peace and although it had been my first visit, I felt as though I'd already been there a thousand times before.

In all of the years that have passed, I haven't changed my mind. In the quiet faraway corner where the orchard meets a wild and overgrown field - that was where I wanted to be - as light and as free as a summer breeze.

'You're probably thinking that I'm crazy?! Why was I thinking about death? Why had I already decided at the age of fifteen where I wanted to be after I died? I don't know what happened. There was just something about that place.'

'I don't think you're crazy Jas. There's nothing wrong with knowing what you want.'

'At fifteen I was looking forward to life. I was quietly excited about all the possibilities that the world had to

offer. I was going to go to uni, get a job and travel the world and be free, be so free. Have a life full of freedom where I could go where I wanted to go and do what I wanted to do-' I stopped. 'It's funny isn't it? Ironic really because by the time I was nineteen, I was praying for death, the pain of living had become too much.'

Forty-Seven

Getting In The Way

'Yeah! Hip-hip-hooray! Yes!' Bursting with happiness, I exited the exam hall with the rest of my year. We'd just finished sitting our final GCSE exam.

'No more revision!'

'No more studying!'

We all spilled out into the playground, exiting the school grounds and going off into different directions.

I called out cheery goodbyes to my school friends. I'd spent five years with them and I believed after the summer holidays, like me, that they would all return to the sixth form at Alumwell.

But as I slowly ambled home, I didn't know that I'd never see some of them ever again. They were taking a different path to mine: some were off to college, some would go straight on the dole and others would be heading into jobs. It was the middle of the afternoon when I arrived home and the house sounded wonderfully quiet.

My uncle Manjeet had been released from prison, so my aunt Harjit and my three cousins had returned to their house in Bentley. My grandfather had died, my masi had married and moved to Leicester and not liking England much, my mother's brother Joshan had returned to India. Only Bibi remained with us.

I couldn't have been happier that after almost six years of disorder, chaos and misfortune - life was peaceful and routine again.

'How was your exam?' My mother asked as soon as I walked into the living room.

'It was ok. Can I go to the library and get some new books?'

My mother shook her head. 'You can go with your sisters at the weekend.'

'But that's ages away!'

On her way out to the kitchen, my mother paused. 'Jas, you're sixteen now and you'll have to learn that there are more important things in life than reading!'

I gave a sharp intake of breath - more important things in my life than reading! That would be the worst thing to ever happen to me! Worse than when I fell into stinging nettles, worse than when I fell out of a tree, worse than when I accidentally swallowed a fly while I was running, worse than the time I thought I saw some fluff on the carpet and picked it up only to find out that it was actually a spider and worse than when I went to pick some flowers and ended up with both my hands covered in dog poo!

'There's never going to be anything more important than reading, mother!' I muttered the words under my breath in case my mother heard and stopped to give me one of her never-ending searing lectures. Both my parents and Bibi had an amazing ability to lecture me and my sisters about the same thing over and over, again and again - they never seemed to tire of repeating the same thing to us a million times.

Slowly I walked upstairs. As I changed out of my school uniform for the very last time, I felt Mama's presence. Relishing her visit, I stood still. She left after a few minutes, leaving me completely happy. Come September, I would be in the sixth form at Alumwell. I'd be able to study English to my heart's content without all of the other dreaded subjects like science and geography getting in the way. And after my 'A' levels, I'd go to university to study journalism and after that I'd go straight to Fleet Street and become a journalist. I hummed as I skipped down the stairs to monopolise the television before any of my sisters returned from school.

I had one more job to do before I could officially start my summer holidays. In a house full of people and chores, it was rare that I ever got the luxury of having the only good mirror in the house all to myself, but with everyone else at school or at work and my mother bustling about in the kitchen, there was no one that I had to elbow out of the way.

I stood in front of the mirror in the living room. While my sisters, cousins and school friends had all outgrown their pigtails by junior school and changed and experimented with different hairstyles, as much as they'd been allowed to by their parents, I had decided that I'd only change my hairstyle at the age of sixteen and I'd stubbornly stuck to wearing my long hair in two pigtails.

Taking one of my long pigtails, I pulled the elastic band off the end of the hair and quickly unraveled the plait. Then I did the same with my other pigtail. I ruffled up my hair as it fell in long waves down my back.

My braces had been removed a few months earlier, but even after two years of treatment my teeth were still not straight. My orthodontist, Mrs Letts had mixed up my dental records with those of another patient with the same name. She was so incompetent that she had never even noticed her error at my monthly appointments, clearly not even paying enough attention when I was in her chair. She only discovered her mistake at my last appointment and she didn't suggest any remedy or treatment, simply laughing it off and hurrying me out of her practice. Believing there was nothing that I or anyone else could do and not wanting to worry my parents, I didn't even tell them about her mistake.

Despite my imperfect smile, I still felt happy as I twirled in front of the mirror - job done and quickly bored of my reflection, I switched on the television.

'I had it all mapped out in front of me - 'A' levels and then university and then work as a journalist. But I was so stupid.'

'Jas, did you forget how your family had treated all of your aunts as soon as they were old enough to be legally married?'

I shook my head. 'I didn't forget. But I shoved it to the back of my mind because things were different in my family, with my parents. They were more easy-going than my grandfather and uncles. Me and my sisters were encouraged in our education by my parents. Dimple was studying at Walsall College, the first girl in our family to go onto further education so I believed that our lives would go in a different direction to my aunts. I forgot that in my family, marriage is more important than anything else...even education and a career. I forgot that in the eyes of the Sikh Punjabi community and my parents, if as a girl I'm worth nothing, then how can my dreams be worth anything?'

Forty-Eight

Start Running

'Ramon has invited us to her house and he wants me to go with him,' said my mother to Bibi. 'I've tried to explain to him that both of us don't need to go. He can go on his own, can't he? Why does he need to drag me there? I can't go in my state! Do you think I'll look good sitting there with my big belly? No...no! I'm not going!' Heavily pregnant with her seventh child, adamant my mother shook her head.

In a bid to get Bibi to take his side, my dad turned to her. 'Bibi, explain to your daughter that I can't very well go on my own now, can I? Ramon specifically asked that we both attend. It's only down the road in Wolverhampton, we'll be there and back in no time. We don't have to stay long.'

My aunt Ramon was hosting a religious ceremony in her home and like my uncle Manjeet, her and her husband Satpal were Khalsa Sikhs. She was also my aunt Pupinder's sister-in-law. Ramon's husband Satpal and Pupinder's husband Manvir were brothers and as such Ramon was considered a noteworthy relative.

Bibi, who didn't like to be stuck in the middle of my parents' disagreements, would if pushed usually side with my dad, but not today. 'She can't go anywhere looking like that,' Bibi said quietly.

Knowing instantly that if he didn't have Bibi, he had lost the argument, my dad sighed. 'Well, someone else needs to go with me then because I don't want to go on my own. Why don't you come with me Bibi?'

Bibi shook her head. 'What am I going to do there? Why don't you take one or two of the girls?'

My mother immediately jumped on the idea. 'That's a thought! Now why didn't I think of that myself? Take two of the girls!'

When my parents had started bickering about going to Ramon's house, Sarb and I were the only girls in the living room.

My dad turned to my sister. 'Sarb, do you want to go with me to Ramon's house?'

My sister who was always ready to be sociable, nodded her head. Needing another, my dad looked around and spied me reading in the corner. 'Jas?'

Bibi tutted. 'She won't go! Just ask one of the other girls instead!'

Unless it was a close family function, preferring to stay at home and read, I refused to visit relatives or attend social functions and my parents knew that they'd have to practically drag me out of the house if they wanted me to go anywhere.

But my dad was desperate enough to try. 'Jas, do you want to come with me and Sarb. We won't stay long.'

I looked up. 'Ok, I'll go,' I said, closing my book.

There was a surprised silence that I'd agreed to go and so easily at that. But just in case I changed my mind, my mother and Bibi quickly pulled out Indian clothes for me and Sarb and hurried us out of the front door with my dad. We departed with their advice ringing in our ears, 'be polite and courteous at all times, do whatever you're asked to do and help out.'

When we arrived at Ramon's house, our cousins and our other aunts and uncles greeted us with delight. Ramon led us upstairs to the Guru Granth Sahib and Sarb and I sat listening to the prayers until my dad nodded at us, giving us permission to leave the prayer room.

Downstairs Ramon's daughter Henna was waiting impatiently for us to join her and she dragged us out into the garden. Seating us at the garden table, Ramon fussed over us, trying to feed me and Sarb all manner of Indian treats before she returned to the kitchen where the rest of the women were working.

As Sarb and I laughed with Henna in the warm afternoon sunshine, I felt great. I was in the company of my lovely cousin, the stress of my GCSE exams was over and a carefree summer stretched out in front of me with my return to sixth form to look forward to in early September.

'You're back? Where have you guys been?' Henna asked, looking past me.

I glanced over my shoulder to see who she was talking to. Three boys had walked into the back garden. Recognising Henna's two younger brothers, I smiled at them, but I couldn't place the third boy, a tall teenager. I turned back around as he threw himself into the chair opposite.

'None of your business Henna!' He tilted his head to one side as he spoke. Set below thick eyebrows, his big brown eyes were flanked with the thickest and longest eyelashes that I'd ever seen on a boy. His nose was straight and his cheekbones showed off his chiselled jawline and wide lips.

Without doubt, he was one of the best-looking boys that I'd ever seen, but there was an unmistakable arrogance dancing in his eyes. In an instant I knew two things: he was aware of how good-looking he was and I didn't like him.

Hardly blinking he stared at me. 'Alright, I'm Jay.'

'Hi,' I said as I remembered who he was. He was the youngest son of Manjit - Satpal and Manvir's sister. I'd met him several years earlier when my parents and Dimple had gone to India and Sarb and I had stayed at my aunt Pupinder's house in Birmingham.

Jay's family had lived at the top of Pupinder's street, but shortly after my stay in Birmingham, his family had moved to Vancouver. However Jay's father Ranbir hadn't liked life in Vancouver and he'd returned to England alone, living in the family home which they'd kept and hadn't sold, he'd opened a taxi company. Jay and his mother Manjit would come to visit him. They were staying for the summer holidays before they returned to Canada.

Jay was chatting with Sarb and Henna, but his eyes kept drifting back to me. Not joining in the conversation, I sat listening quietly. But uncomfortable with Jay's constant gaze, I got up to leave.

'Where you going?' asked Jay.

Surprised and annoyed that someone I barely knew was asking me where I was going, I frowned but saying nothing, I turned and left.

Believing that I would be safe from Jay's stare, I walked into the kitchen where the women were working, but he quickly followed me inside.

As he walked into the kitchen, his eyes were already searching for me. Uneasy, I left the kitchen and went into the living room, but without a word Jay followed me into there as well. I sighed as I turned around and headed back to the kitchen. All the women, including Jay's mother Manjit looked up as I re-entered the kitchen and seeing him behind me again, they exchanged amused glances amongst themselves as they tried to hide their smiles.

I stood awkwardly in the kitchen, unsure of what to do next. I just wanted to get away from Jay's stare. Then to my relief, my dad walked into the kitchen.

Greeting the women one by one, he told Ramon that it was time we were leaving.

But before anyone else could say anything, Jay spoke out. 'Can't you stay a little bit longer uncle?'

I was startled at Jay's outspokenness and it seemed like my dad was too because he was momentarily lost for words, but seizing the opportunity, Ramon and the rest of the women all rounded on my dad.

'You must stay!'

'You can't go yet!'

'We've hardly had any time with you and the girls.'

Suddenly surrounded and hounded by the insistence of several loud women, my dad could barely be heard over the noise as he tried to insist that we had to leave. As he continued to insist, the women changed their pleas.

'Well, at least leave the girls here then.'

'Yes, leave Sarb and Jas here for the night.'

'They rarely ever get to spend any time with their cousins, you're always so busy!'

'Leave them with us for tonight.'

Hearing the commotion from the garden, Sarb and my cousins walked into the kitchen. When my young cousins also began begging and pleading, in lieu of any instructions from my mother, my dad caved.

As collective squeals of delight and big smiles filled the room, I suddenly felt a strong urge to start running. Feeling as if I was being hunted, all the hairs on the back of my neck stood up, but I shrugged off the feeling as I watched my dad drive away.

Returning to the garden with Sarb and my cousins I tried to relax. Luckily, Jay left me alone. He spent much of the rest of the day engaged in conversation with his mother Manjit, his grandmother and Ramon.

That evening, two strange things happened. Jay's mother, Manjit insisted that Sarb and I dance for her. We hesitated, Ramon's religious ceremony wasn't the kind of occasion where dancing was appropriate, but remembering our mother's instructions, 'do whatever you're asked to do' and not feeling that we could refuse her request and with Ramon's encouragement, we reluctantly obliged. Not allowed to watch us dancing, Jay and our male cousins were banished to the garden, while the women watched and clapped along to the music.

Then later when Jay's father Ranbir arrived at Ramon's house, grinning Manjit led him over to where Sarb and I were sitting in the garden. Completely ignoring my sister, Ranbir proceeded to ask me a series of questions.

'I don't work . . . I'm still at school . . . I'm going to start my 'A' levels in September . . . I've just turned sixteen,' I answered in quick succession.

Smiling Ranbir stood silently studying me for a few moments, before he turned and disappeared into the house.

I smiled apologetically at Sarb as we shrugged off his odd behaviour.

Early the following morning, my dad returned to collect me and Sarb. Relieved to be home, I picked up my book exactly where I'd left it, pushing the strange events at Ramon's house out of my mind.

But later that day, my mother received a telephone call from my aunt Pupinder, who didn't beat around the bush. She explained that Jay's parents had wanted to speak to my dad about his daughters and it was unfortunate that he'd picked us up and left before they'd had a chance to talk with him. She ended the call by telling my mother that my dad needed to call her as soon as he returned home.

My mother hung up the telephone and then turned to me and Sarb. 'What did you two do?'

'Nothing!'

'Nothing!'

We replied in unison.

My mother narrowed her eyes at us, but before she could say or do anything else, Sarb and I quickly exited the living room. While Sarb disappeared through the kitchen door, I headed into the front room. It was a tactic that my sisters and I had perfected - my mother would have to choose which of us to go after and in her moment of indecision, we'd all be out of her reach.

Who knew what Pupinder wanted! Our behaviour at Ramon's house had been impeccable and I didn't need an ear bashing from my mother for no good reason.

After my dad returned home, as my mother hovered anxiously at his elbow, he called Pupinder. He finished the call and then briefly glanced over at me before he turned to my mother.

'It's nothing, there's no need to worry.' And with that, my dad walked into the kitchen for his daily can of beer, but this time my mother followed him.

There wasn't much my parents said out of earshot of us girls so I knew that whatever it was, it was probably something serious. Maybe Ramon was upset that my mother had missed her religious ceremony, maybe she had been disappointed that my mother had sent her daughters in her place instead, maybe Ramon and Pupinder had wanted to hold a special prayer for my mother in the hope that she'd have a son this time round, but they hadn't been able to because my mother hadn't gone to Ramon's house. I tried to focus on my homework, but I had a nagging feeling that Pupinder's phone call was something to do with me. But I quickly shrugged off the thought, dismissing it because I wasn't important enough for anyone to spend their time thinking about me.

'I always believed that my parents would consider me first before they thought of anyone else. That they would think what's best for their child, what does their child want. But that's a very stupid and naive way of thinking.'

'Is it Jas? A lot of parents do protect their children and put them first.'

'That's the way it should be, but I wasn't lucky when it came to matching parents to children. Ultimately, I was like a stupid dumb-dumb believing that the phone call and the quiet chat between my parents in the kitchen was to do with the imminent arrival of a new baby.'

Forty-Nine

Itchy Threads

'It's another bag,' said Pardeep as she closed the front door and carried the plastic bag into the living room. She set it down in front of Bibi and my mother.

Bibi reached for the bag, opened it, turned it upside down and shook out the contents, spilling baby clothes onto the carpet.

My mother had taken several vows that if God granted her a son: she would walk in her bare feet to Pleck gurdwara (she did), she would plant a tree (she did) and that she would only dress the boy in second-hand cast offs for the first year of his life (and she did). After my brother Kiran was born, my mother remained true to her word and only dressed my brother in clothes that had been donated by neighbours, friends, relatives and even strangers who'd heard the story of the boy born after six daughters.

A time of rejoicing and heartfelt thanks to God, who according to all of my female relatives - 'can be late, but he always delivers.' Everyone shared in my parents' happiness and the house was flooded with well-wishers, friends and relatives who came from far and wide - all pausing in the kitchen to eat the customary serving of sugar before going near the new baby.

My brother Kiran had a mass of black hair, big brown eyes and the cutest button nose. He was a happy and content baby. Fussed over and adored, there were too many hands and not enough baby to go around. The women cooed as they laughed and smiled, their eager hands twitching to hold my brother.

My brother was barely four weeks old when my mother handed me a rakhri made up of bright red and orange decorative threads plaited together.

Every year my sisters and I had to tie rakhris onto the wrists of our cousin brothers, but I disliked the meaning behind the old Indian tradition. A sister ties a colourful thread onto the wrist of her brother to ward off evil and protect him and in turn he promises to protect her and her honour. The undertones of rakhri were that a girl cannot look after herself and had to rely on her brothers and cousin brothers for protection.

Maybe this year, I would feel differently about rakhri because I now had a brother of my own.

Beaming my mother was certainly very excited and happy about it. 'See girls, this rakhri you don't need to run around after Sonny and his brothers or anyone else!'

After Dimple had tied a rakhri on Kiran, it was my turn. I gingerly sat down on the settee next to him as he lay sleeping. My baby brother couldn't even lift his own head and I had to bite my lip to stop myself from yelling out to everyone about how ridiculous it was that this baby was supposed to protect me! But not wanting to upset my mother, I gently tied the thread around my brother's tiny little wrist, silently apologizing to him, because no baby wants itchy threads tied around their tiny wrist.

'These rituals and ceremonies are all encouraged by women. Probably because it's much easier to pass

responsibility onto someone else to look after you rather than rely on yourself and be strong enough to stand on your own two feet.'

'That can be said for a lot of women from a lot of different cultures Jas.'

'True...but the Indian culture is one of these cultures, although I'm sure that there are others too - that has actual rituals which actively encourage and reinforce the idea that women need to have a man to protect them. It gives a man free reign to check up on his sister's behaviour and interfere with her life under the guise that he's looking after her and her honour. It's just another form of control. Fathers, brothers and then husbands, all form a line of control where they pass their control of the woman along to the next male in line. If the father dies then the brother will automatically assume control over his sisters and then after she's married, her husband will control her.'

Fifty

Seed Of My Depression

'Oh my god! There you are!' I squealed with delight as I embraced Maria and Roshna. Spotting some of our other friends across the room, we rushed over to join them. Brimming with happiness and laughter, we all caught up with each other's summer news. Mine about the birth of my baby brother produced a fresh round of excited squeals and hugs.

It was a beautiful September day and I was back at Alumwell. Only this time I was a first year in sixth form. While some of my friends were retaking their GCSEs, with the exception of maths, I wasn't doing any retakes. It hadn't come as a surprise to anyone, least of all me, that I'd failed my maths miserably. It didn't matter though, I'd still get to spend the majority of my time studying 'A' level history and English literature.

As sixth formers, we no longer had to wear school uniform. We had our own large room to study and hang around in during the day so unlike the rest of the students, we were no longer at the mercy of the outside elements. We were allowed to have our dinner first before the rest of the school and permitted to jump the dinner queue if we wanted. We were free to leave the school premises whenever we chose and best of all, we were no longer under the constant gaze of our teachers, who mostly left us to our own devices. It was those small things that made for a carefree and joyful time as we slowly adjusted to becoming independent.

A few days later, as I walked home from school with my sisters, I was lost in my daydreams about Romeo and Juliet. I'd just started studying it with the rest of my English class. My English teacher, Mr Jacobs was already a firm favourite of mine and I loved his lessons.

As soon as I walked in through the back door, I was greeted by my mother. 'We're going over to Manjit's house. She's returning to Vancouver in two days. They keep asking to see you . . . do you want to go?'

Not fancying a trip to Birmingham, I screwed up my nose. 'Nah, I don't wanna go.'

'Leave Jas here,' said my dad as he came down the stairs. 'We're taking Dimple with us. The three of us is more than enough, we don't want to cause a rabble at Manjit's house.'

After leaving instructions with Bibi that my younger sisters and I weren't allowed to stay up late on a school night, my parents left with Dimple. They returned so late into the night that I didn't even hear them come in.

The following morning as we rushed around getting ready for school, my mother ordered us all to promptly return home as soon as school finished. None of us wanted a whack so we didn't remind her that that's what we did every day anyway. I was almost out of the back door when my mother stopped me.

'Err . . . Jas . . . Jay is coming to see you today,' she said, throwing me a nervous smile.

I stopped and spun around. My younger sisters all paused and they looked just as confused as I did.

'Jay's coming here?' I asked.

My mother didn't look me in the eye. 'Oh shut up . . . he's coming to look at you and that's that!'

My sisters looked bewildered at my mother's tone as I suddenly felt a strange panic. We all knew what it meant when 'a boy came to look at you.'

Several months earlier, a boy and his family had come to our house to see if Dimple could be a possible match for marriage. But Dimple had been asked beforehand whether it was ok for the boy to come and see her with a view to marriage. She had happily agreed. With the middle person between our two families arranging a date for the meeting, we had known for several weeks, giving us all time to prepare. Cooking and cleaning before the boy and his family had turned up on our doorstep on a quiet Saturday afternoon.

After the introductions had been made and tea and samosas served and eaten, Dimple and the boy had been left on their own to talk, though I had to remain in the room with them. My mother had decided that even though both his family and my family had only retreated a few feet away to the front room, Dimple and this boy still needed a chaperone. I was annoyed at their backward thinking, narrow-minded set-up and the boy must have been too because the marriage proposal didn't materialise and nothing more was made of it.

I frowned. It was a school night and no one had asked me if it was ok if Jay came to look at me. I wasn't even thinking about marriage. I wasn't going to marry him. I wasn't going to marry anyone. I was going to university to become a journalist. Jay had already made me feel hounded at Ramon's house, now I just wanted to be left alone. Annoyed that my parents had already made plans for him to come over without asking me first, I opened my mouth to protest to my mother, but then thinking better of it, I closed it again.

I didn't need to waste any time or energy trying to persuade my mother. Jay's parents and my parents were clearly thinking something about me and Jay, but that didn't mean that we had to agree to their plans. Jay's parents could just be making him come to see me because they liked my parents and felt sorry for them because they had six daughters. Jay might not even have got a say on whether or not, he actually wanted to come and see me. This could just be something that he was having to do to please his parents. Going to 'look at a girl' didn't mean that anything had been decided, agreed or that it was a done deal. As I walked to school with my sisters, I thought that once we were left alone, without our families around, we could turn each other down and nothing should be made of it.

Silently I consoled myself. In an arranged marriage the boy's family and the girl's family allow the boy and the girl a chance to speak to each other, while the families wait in the other room - that's what had happened with Dimple. Sometimes the boy and the girl only get a few minutes alone before they had to decide whether they wanted to marry each other. Sometimes in sensible families, the boy and the girl would be allowed to spend as much time together as they needed before they made a decision, no one was rushed or pressured. But I wouldn't need any time, I already knew what my answer was going to be.

I could only hope, like Dimple and that boy, that once Jay and I talked with each other without everyone else around and he and I both mutually agreed that we didn't want to get married and marriage wasn't right for us, our parents would understand and accept our decision. After all, I'd only just turned sixteen and he was still only fifteen.

But as I turned into the grounds of my school, I sensed my grandmother Mama beside me and suddenly I felt the urge to run. She was urging me to run and not stop. To keep running until I was far away from school, my house, Walsall town and all of my relatives, including my parents. As Mama left, I pushed the panic down and shrugged myself off. I was being stupid, I wasn't the only girl in the world who had a boy coming to see her. Unexpected though this was, it was just a process that I had to go through today. Jay was coming tonight to see me, I would speak with him and say no . . . no thank you and by tomorrow all this would be done and dusted and I could carry on with my life as I'd planned.

In the afternoon as I left school and walked home with my sisters, I'd almost forgotten about Jay's visit. Walking in through the back door, I felt myself pass by Mama. I paused, it was very unusual for me to sense Mama twice in one day. I couldn't understand why she was just outside the doorway. But as I continued into the house, the last thing I expected to encounter was bedlam. Our tiny terrace was crammed full of neighbours and relatives, it was more crowded than I'd ever seen it before and people seemed to be rushing around everywhere.

As soon as I walked into the living room, I was pounced on.

'Ah, Jas is here!'

'Everyone! Jas is here!'

'She's back from school!'

I frowned. Since when did my return home from school warrant a special announcement?

'Go and get changed girls,' said my mother to my sisters before she turned to me. 'Jas, you need to wear your best Indian suit. Go upstairs, I've already laid it out for you on your bed. Hurry up now.'

'What's going on? Why are all these people here?' I asked her.

But my mother had already departed in the direction of the kitchen. Not answering me or even turning around, she was lost in the bustle of people milling around. Even relatives from Birmingham and Wolverhampton were here.

When the boy had come to see Dimple, the house hadn't been crowded with neighbours and relatives.

Apart from the boy's family, no one else had been present and the house had been orderly, calm and quiet. With all these relatives around, how were Jay and I going to get a chance to sit and speak together just on our own, like we were supposed to? Maybe some of the relatives would go and sit in the front room or step outside into the garden.

Feeling confused, I joined Sarb and Pardeep upstairs. One of my cousins was sent up to hurry us along and throwing on my best Indian suit, I went back downstairs. Dodging all the relatives milling around, I headed straight to the kitchen which was already crowded and overrun with relatives. There were bound to be chores to do and with a sigh of relief, I noted that it wasn't my turn to do the dishes.

'Ah Jas . . . how pretty you look,' said my aunt Bhav as she walked into the kitchen. She took both of my hands in hers and gave me a wide smile. 'You've turned into such a beautiful girl.'

Astonished at her words, I stared at her in surprise. Bhav had never even looked in my direction before, let alone given me a compliment. I blushed. 'Err...thanks.'

'They're here!' Shouted someone from within the house.

'Jay and his family are here!'

I was beginning to feel a strange sense of suffocation. The hairs on the back of my neck stood up and I suddenly wanted to be in an open park somewhere, standing in my bare feet on the green grass, instead of being in our overcrowded and cramped kitchen in Walsall.

Dimple walked into the kitchen with a smirk plastered across her face and I knew immediately that she knew something and that whatever it was that she knew, I really ought to know it too.

'Dimple, what's going on? Why're all these people here?'

Shrugging she laughed. 'I don't know . . . how would I know? Why don't you go inside and find out for yourself why all these people are here!'

Not for the first time in my life, I really wanted to thump my older sister, but as I stood in the kitchen becoming increasingly uneasy and worried, I became aware that the noise level in the house had settled to a quiet hum. That meant Jay's family were now inside our house.

In my naivety and confusion, I had overlooked something: all of my relatives were jolly and happy, appearing to be celebrating an occasion, though no occasion had happened yet. That should have alerted me to something being amiss.

I knew that something wasn't right, but I tried not to panic. I knew how it was supposed to go. I'd get a chance to speak to Jay on his own and I could tell him that my answer was no. Maybe after he saw me again he'd say no. Of course! At school I'd been rejected by every boy that I'd liked, Jay would be no different. In fact, he was so good–looking he could get any girl he wanted so why would he settle for me? I just had to wait until I was alone with him and tell him 'no thanks' and I reminded myself that by tomorrow, all this noise and chaos would be a faint and distant memory.

From the living room, I heard my name being called.

My aunt Harjit turned to me. 'Jas, they're calling you. You need to go inside.' She sounded perplexed, as if somehow I'd not heard my own name being called.

I ignored my aunt, but when my name was called again from the living room and I still refused to move, the nerves and confusion of the other people standing in the kitchen began to show.

Sarb and Pardeep glanced at me nervously. 'Jas, I think they're calling you.'

Not wanting to walk into the living room, I didn't reply. I was desperately trying to push down the feeling of wanting to run out of the back door.

'Ah! There you are Jas!' My cousin Japdeep barged into the kitchen, shoving and elbowing people aside in her haste. She'd been sent to the kitchen to fetch me. 'Come on, everyone's been waiting for you!' She grabbed me by my shoulder and half-pushed, half-steered me through the crowded kitchen and mass of people until I was standing in the middle of the living room.

As I stumbled to a standstill, I couldn't see my parents anywhere, but what I did see made my blood run cold.

Two chairs had been placed into the middle of the crowded room - Jay was sitting in one. The other chair was empty. I knew exactly what it meant if a boy and a girl were being seated side by side and I hadn't agreed to anything - I hadn't even been asked. This was not the way it was supposed to be. Everyone was supposed to clear out and Jay and I were supposed to have a talk with each other and everyone had to wait to hear what we'd decided to do. Somewhere in the process, a couple of steps seemed to have been missed.

I looked around for my parents. They would sort this out and move the chairs so that I wasn't sitting right next to Jay. Obviously there had been an error by some relative who'd placed two chairs in the middle of the room like this. But surely all my relatives knew by now that when 'a boy comes to see a girl' how it's actually supposed to work? Certainly it wasn't like this!

'Jas sit on that chair,' said one of my aunts.

I didn't move. I couldn't simply go and sit down next to Jay - nothing had been said or decided between us.

'Sit down. That empty chair is for you Jas.'

I still didn't move.

Someone chuckled. 'Go on, there's no need to be shy.'

I remained standing.

Trying not to panic, I arched myself up onto my tiptoes. 'Mum?' I tried to look over peoples' heads, but either my mother or my dad were anywhere to be seen. I tried again. 'Mum!'

'Your mum was just here. Where's she gone? She must be coming,' said one of my aunts. 'Never mind Jas, you just sit down, you don't need to wait for your mum.'

But I didn't sit down. Instead I turned to Japdeep and trying to keep my voice steady, I whispered. 'Where's my mum?'

'I don't know, she was just here.' Japdeep turned and called out into the crowd of people. 'Auntie?'

I was acutely aware that every eye in the room was on me and as I looked for a way out of the living room, I realised that everyone was packed in so tightly that I'd have to ask people to step aside and move out of my way. From their expectant faces, I knew that no one was simply going to move aside and make room for me to go through the crowd.

There was a shift in the faces of my relatives as some of them started to mutter.

'Why isn't she sitting down?'

'That chair is for you Jas, you're allowed to sit on it!'

'There's no need to wait for your mother or to be shy! Just sit down.'

I heard them, but I didn't want to sit down.

'Sit down,' said Jay's mother Manjit.

I still didn't move.

Wanting to score points with the adults in the room and exasperated with my continued refusal to sit down, my cousin Japdeep turned to me. 'Jas! Just sit down!' And before I could do or say anything, Japdeep pushed me towards the empty chair.

The push was forceful and unexpected. Falling and tripping forwards, I stumbled and losing my balance, I fell down heavily onto both knees, landing squarely at Jay's feet.

Since I'd entered the living room, Jay was the one person who I'd avoided looking at, but I'd landed right under his nose.

As the room erupted into laughter at my fall, grinning Jay leaned down and gently took me by both shoulders. His touch was so tender that I was stunned into silence and as effortlessly as one picks up a toy doll, Jay lifted me up and carefully placed me onto the empty chair next to him.

Humiliated by my fall, confused and unhappy about what was happening, I was grateful that my chunni was partially covering my face as I sat with my head down. As relatives gathered in even closer, both of my parents suddenly appeared out of thin air.

'What's happening?' I whispered to Sarb as she managed to elbow herself to the front of the crowd.

She frowned. 'I think you're getting engaged Jas,' she said.

'Your parents couldn't face you. They knew that they'd done the wrong thing.'

'I know. I came so close to physically pushing people out of the way so that I could get out of that room.'

'You didn't though, did you? Because you'd been raised first and foremost to be a dutiful daughter. You were conditioned to put your parents' wishes first and not to do anything to humiliate or embarrass them or to create a scene and upset people – because that would never do.'

'Yep, I gave my parents loyalty and respect when they didn't deserve any. And instead of using my mouth to tell everyone to piss off, which is what I should have done, I kept my mouth shut and let whatever was happening happen. I couldn't process it anyway. It was like it was me, but not me, sitting there next to Jay, getting engaged at the age of sixteen. You can have all the Christmas dinners you want, watch Dallas, eat meat and drink and not wear a turban, let your daughters dance and tell them to do their homework and repeat a hundred times to them about the importance of education, but at the very centre of my parents' hearts lay a backward small Punjabi village mentality. When I fell to the ground, the seed of my

depression was sown. When I fell, I just kept on falling for years and years after that day. I always thought that someone would save me, someone would come along and they would stop me from falling. Maybe the flicker would turn up, but no one came. After that day, every happy event in my life would be overshadowed. I came to hate surprises. I don't even care if it's a nice surprise. I won't even have my ipod on shuffle, that's how much I hate surprises. But my parents hadn't quite finished surprising me yet . . . all those years and I'd had no idea that when I was only six months old, still a baby, my parents had promised me in marriage to Jay.'

Dear Reader,

Thank you for reading my book. If you enjoyed it, please leave a review on Amazon, I'd really appreciate it and your review will help other readers to discover my books.

My memoirs are primarily written to help inspire and empower women. A lot of women will relate to many of the issues I discuss in my storytelling. Perhaps a woman who you know will be able to take some comfort from knowing that they're not alone and that someone else has also endured and survived similar experiences so please spread the word and share this book with your friends and family.

If you liked ***Spare Burden***, then you'll love the next book in the **Life Out Of Reach** series, ***Not The Property Of*** (to be published in Spring 2021) and ***Searching For Breath*** (to be released in Autumn 2021).

Please sign up at www.jasdosanjh.com to receive my occasional newsletter or follow me for pre-launch notifications about new books, workshops, training, online courses and speaking events.

Twitter:	www.twitter.com/JasDosanjh73
Facebook:	www.facebook.com/jasdosanjh.334
Instagram:	www.instagram.com/jasdosanjh73
LinkedIn:	www.linkedin.com/in/jasdosanjh73
Website:	www.jasdosanjh.com

Printed in Great Britain
by Amazon

60587991R00160